HOW TO EAT AN
ELEPHANT

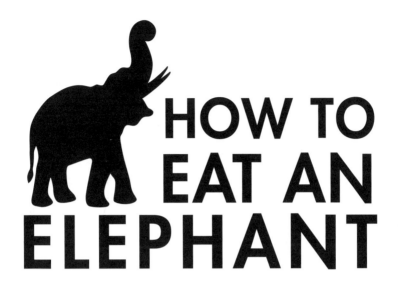

HOW TO EAT AN ELEPHANT

ACHIEVING FINANCIAL SUCCESS
ONE BITE AT A TIME

Frank Wiginton

John Wiley & Sons Canada, Ltd.

For general information about our other products and services, please contact our Customer Care Department within Canada at (800) 567-4797, outside Canada at (416) 236-4433 or fax (416) 236-8743.

Wiley publishes in a variety of print and electronic formats and by print-on-demand. Some material included with standard print versions of this book may not be included in e-books or in print-on-demand. If this book refers to media such as a CD or DVD that is not included in the version you purchased, you may download this material at http://booksupport.wiley.com. For more information about Wiley products, visit www.wiley.com.

Library and Archives Canada Cataloguing in Publication Data

Wiginton, Frank, 1975–
How to eat an elephant : achieving financial success one bite at a time/Frank Wiginton.
Issued also in electronic formats
ISBN 978-1-118-45973-7
1. Finance, Personal. I. Title.
HG179.W528 2012 332.024 C2012-906038-0

9781118459805 (ebk); 9781118459799 (ebk); 9781118459782 (ebk)

Production Credits
Managing Editor: Alison Maclean
Executive Editor: Karen Milner
Production Editor: Pauline Ricablanca
Cover Design: Adrian So
Composition: Laserwords
Printer: Dickinson Press

Printed in the United States

1 2 3 4 5 DP 16 15 14 13 12

To my wife Diane, for believing in me before there was something to believe in. Without your love and support, none of this would be possible.

CONTENTS

ACKNOWLEDGEMENTS

This book and its online tools would not have been possible without substantial help and support from many people. A very special thank you to my wife and project manager, Diane. Without her expertise, this project may have taken years, if not decades, to complete. To my parents who always encouraged me to try, even if the task was difficult, and for instilling in me the values of wanting to help others and contribute to society. To my friends at TriDelta Financial who have provided guidance and encouragement on many facets of this book and its tools.

HOW TO USE THIS GUIDE

THIS BOOK WAS WRITTEN AS a guide to take you through a step-by-step process to get your finances in order. Each chapter can be read on its own but you may find it easier to follow (and achieve greater success) by following the book in sequence, from Chapter 1 to 12.

If you spend just four hours of one day each month reading the chapter and doing the exercises online, you will have the majority of your personal finances in order in one year.

If personal finance is not really your favourite topic, you are in luck! This guide is designed to take you through the process in small, manageable, bite-sized pieces to help you ensure success. Follow these simple steps to get all your personal finances in order:

Step One: Read one chapter each month.

Step Two: Make notes in a journal or write in the book itself as you read each chapter.

Step Three: Log into the website at www.howtoeatanelephant.ca and complete the exercises for that chapter.

Step Four: Once you have completed the exercises, download your report.

Step Five: Schedule time next month to complete the next chapter.

Step Six: Reward yourself for accomplishing that month's work!

Once you've completed all 12 chapters and all the exercises online, download a copy of your summary financial report and spend some time reviewing it.

Many events and changes can happen in a year, so you may need to go back and review some of the tools and exercises to update them with the latest information. You may wish to repeat this entire process every couple of years or following a major life change. Take a copy of your summary report to a certified financial planner who will help you prepare a comprehensive financial plan. These documents are required and can save the planner a lot of time and you a lot of money.

This first step will be the beginning of an important partnership that will help you develop solutions and ideas to increase your overall wealth, reduce your financial risk, reduce your taxation, and ultimately provide you with a better quality of life!

INTRODUCTION

How do you eat an elephant?
One bite at a time!

MANY TIMES IN LIFE WE are faced with a task we don't like, or a task that is difficult to manage because of its size. By learning what needs to be done and then doing it in small, bite-sized pieces, we can complete these tasks successfully and reach our goals.

People make financial planning and management out to be a huge task. They tend to get discouraged and quickly feel overwhelmed. Unfortunately, they believe they don't have the confidence, knowledge, and ability to do it. They have less and less trust in those giving advice because of the constant sales pitches and a lack of real, unbiased advice from so-called "advisors."

For many years now, when clients have approached me to prepare a financial plan, I have asked them to pull together a variety of documents in order to prepare a comprehensive financial plan. These documents give me important information about their financial situation and what they would like to achieve. Clients often feel that the amount of work they need to do and the quantity of information they need to pull together are overwhelming!

To help them overcome this fear and stress, about 10 years ago I started breaking down the information needed from my clients into much smaller, more manageable, bite-sized pieces. When they came to me and said, "Oh my goodness! That seems like a lot of work!" I would ask them to do one exercise and return that information to me. When I got that back, I would then give them the next exercise to do and ask them to return that to me. Over time, and after a series of exercises, I would eventually accumulate the necessary information to prepare their comprehensive financial plan.

As I work with people and help them with their personal finances, I find that many of them don't have the most basic aspects of their personal finances in order. The number of misconceptions and misunderstandings about some of the fundamental tools and resources, including products, continues to surprise me. But now this book will finally give you, the reader, the information and tools to do it on your own, or at the very least to learn how to get organized and find someone to help you. I have provided step-by-step instructions in plain language with stories about others who have achieved financial and personal milestones, and most importantly, unbiased, independent advice that you can trust, with no sales pitch!

This book and its website (www.howtoeatanelephant.ca) will take you through a series of simple exercises that will get your finances in order and set you on the path to financial success! The only commitment required of you is to spend four hours or less—one day each month—reading a chapter and doing the exercises online. This adds up to approximately 0.5% of your time each month to achieve financial peace of mind, success, and a better quality of life.

As you complete each chapter, a new exercise with instructions, tips and tricks, and additional guidance from me will help to ensure your success. By the end of the book, I hope you will feel empowered, more knowledgeable, and secure in the fact that you have all your finances in order. My hope is that by making it easy to get the fundamentals of your personal finances in order, you will be able to reduce your anxiety and stress levels about personal finances. My only question to you is:

Are you ready for a better quality of life?

PART
ONE

UNDERSTANDING YOUR FINANCES

Laying the Foundation for Financial Success

1

SETTING AND ACHIEVING GOALS

The greatest danger for most of us lies not in setting our aim too high and falling short; but in setting our aim too low, and achieving our mark.

—Michelangelo

IF YOU ASKED MOST PEOPLE if they had goals, almost everyone would say they did. So the real question becomes, why is it that most people don't work toward achieving their goals? The main reason is that their goals aren't in front of them on a daily basis. Another reason is that when they set their goals, they don't do so properly. For example, someone might tell you something like, "I want to go to Hawaii." Although this is a goal, it is not set up properly to be met with success. Let's look at what needs to be done to increase the likelihood that goals will be met.

One Frank Thought

You may be wondering why a personal finance book has goal-setting as the subject of the first chapter. The reason is to help you identify the things that are most important to you so that, when you are making financial decisions later on, your focus and priorities will be on these goals.

Write It Down

The first step, and the biggest, is to write them down. Studies have shown that those who not only make goals but also write them down dramatically increase their chance of success in achieving their goals.

Define It

The second step in setting a goal is to ensure that you have defined all of the components of a goal. You likely have heard the acronym "SMART," which stands for Specific, Measurable, Attainable, Realistic, and Timely. So, the SMART version of the goal mentioned above would look like this: I want to take the family to Hawaii for three weeks, at a cost of $8,000, in two years' time.

You could even take it a step further and say: I want to go to the islands of Kauai, Oahu, and Maui for one week each. It will cost me a total of $8,000. I will need to save $333 a month, and I will be there from February 7 to February 28, 2015.

Specific: Trip to Hawaii for three weeks.
Measurable: Cost is $8,000; time to attain goal is two years.
Attainable: I can save $333 a month; I will have accumulated vacation time; I have no issues with flying or travelling to the United States.
Realistic: I can afford it.
Timely: Two years to plan and execute is sufficient.

So now you can see the difference between just having a goal in your head and having a goal that is SMART. It's now easy to understand that, when a goal is defined properly, the probability of achieving it goes up tremendously.

Setting Your Goals and Yourself Up for Success!

First, I want you to daydream about all the goals you want to attain and the things you want to do. I don't want you to have any restrictions on what goals you set. I want you to dream big! I want you to think about all the different areas of your life and the goals you want to achieve. I want you to be comfortable and not put any restrictions on yourself, because anything is possible: you just have to figure out how to achieve it. So, the first step when setting goals is to *dream big!*

Start by making a list of 50 things you want to do right now. Don't worry about making them specific, measurable, attainable, realistic, or time-specific at this stage. I just want you to dream and write! Your list might look something like this:

- Take a trip to Hawaii
- Buy a new car
- Ask for a raise
- Start a blog
- Spend more time with my family
- Go to the gym at least once a week
- Take my lunch to work every day
- Donate some of my time to my favourite charity
- Get my personal financial situation in order
- Read two books a month
- Get my will done
- Learn to speak Spanish
- Get my master's degree
- Help my children buy a house
- Learn to scuba dive
- . . .

Continue writing down goals. Write as many as you can. Get to 50? Great! If you write down 100 goals, that's even better!

Think about what you want to have, what you want to be, what you want to do, what you want to see, and with whom. What are you passionate about? What do you want to learn? Ask yourself questions such as: Why do I do what I do? What is my life mission? What is the legacy I want to leave? Write down all the different things you want to accomplish. Think about what you want for your family, for yourself, for your health, for your wealth, and for your overall wellness (nutrition, fitness, mental health, and career). Think about self-improvement. Think about spirituality. Think about your career. Think about your favourite charity. Don't put any restrictions on where your thoughts take you.

Once you have your list (and you can always add to it later), you need to start organizing it. The easiest way to do this is to start by identifying the time frame during which you want to accomplish your goals. Give each goal a specific time frame. It could be within the next month, the next year, or the next five, 10, 15, 20, or 25 years. Write down the period within which you want to accomplish each of your goals.

Your list now might look like this:

- Take a trip to Hawaii—2 years
- Buy a new car—4 years
- Ask for a raise—2 weeks
- Start a blog—2 months
- Spend more time with my family—daily
- Go to the gym at least once a week—weekly
- Take my lunch to work—daily
- Donate some of my time to my favourite charity—monthly
- Get my personal financial situation in order once and for all—1 year

Now you are ready to organize your goals in the order of their time frame.

What Is the Financial Cost to Accomplish Your Goals?

The next step is to figure out what the cost is to achieve these goals. This may require a little bit of research on your part to learn and understand what steps are involved. For example, it's easy to say that you want to go to Hawaii in two years' time, but without understanding what's involved and how much it costs, it's going to be difficult to know what you need to do to achieve your goal. Therefore, you may want to speak with a travel agent or spend some time online researching how much such a trip costs. Your time frame and cost estimate might look like this:

- Take a trip to Hawaii—2 years = $8,000
- Buy a new car—4 years = $40,000

- Ask for a raise—2 weeks = $5,200 a year
- Start a blog—2 months = $50 + time
- Spend more time with my family—daily = $0 + time
- Go to the gym at least once a week—weekly = $55
- Take my lunch to work—daily = $0 + time
- Donate some of my time to my favourite charity—monthly = $0 + time
- Get my personal financial situation in order once and for all—1 year = $ variable + time

---

One Frank Thought

Before you can truly say whether a goal is realistic financially, you need to better understand your financial situation. Keep working through the chapters and exercises in this book, and I promise you will know what is and isn't possible.

Identify What You Need to Succeed

Next you need to identify the major things that need to happen to accomplish each goal. At the same time, it would also be a good idea to try to foresee what obstacles might prevent you from achieving these goals.

Going back to the Hawaii example, if you are not a U.S. citizen, you will need to ensure your passport is up-to-date (or maybe even get a passport).You may want to research the best time of year to travel there and check with your boss that you can get the time off. So, let's look at the Hawaii goal all together:

Specific: trip to Hawaii
Measurable: for three weeks
Attainable: up-to-date passport, time off work
Realistic: do we have the time and money? Yes or no
Timely: in two years' time

By now you can see that building a list of goals and writing it down can go a long way toward making your goals become a reality.

Review Your List Regularly

Be sure to keep this list in a handy place where you can review it on a daily or weekly basis. Keeping your goals top of mind helps to motivate you to work toward them continually. Maybe you will keep your list in a journal that you write in each day. Then you could keep it on your nightstand to read over every night or first thing in the morning. Maybe you will stick your list to the fridge door or on the wall beside your desk. One colleague of mine has his as the desktop image on his computer! Wherever you keep it, be sure to update it and add to it on a regular basis.

Share Your Goals with Others

There are three main reasons to do this. First, when you share your goals with family members and friends, the goals become more real. What I mean by this is that you become more accountable because other people now expect you to work toward and accomplish them. The next time you see those people, they may ask what you have learned about your goal. For example, they might ask, "Have you decided which islands in Hawaii you are going to visit?" This kind of community accountability helps you to achieve your goals!

Second, by sharing your goals with others, you can learn from their experience. Many people like to share their thoughts and experiences and offer opinions on how best to achieve goals. Sometimes this can be a deterrent, but many times it can be enlightening and encouraging.

Third, for the most part, when you share your goals with others, they will do one of two things: they will either get on board to help you achieve them or get out of your way. It is highly unlikely that someone will actually try to prevent you from achieving one of your goals. People have their own goals and are too busy to stand in your way. When you share your goals, people may offer useful tips, saying, for example, "Oh, you know who you should talk to?" or "I learned to scuba dive with this company and had a great experience! Call them and talk to Jason. He was wonderful!"

Next thing you know, you are well on your way to accomplishing your goal!

Anna

As part of her New Year's resolution, Anna decided that she was finally going to lose the weight that she had been trying to take off for years. She had tried many strategies in the past; the latest trendy diets, listening to her friends, taking advice from her family, and working with a trainer at three of the mass-market gyms. Although she did see some results, they tended to be minor and never really lasted.

Anna admitted to herself that the lack of results was in part due to her behaviour, but she felt that it was also due to the people from whom she was getting help. In some cases she walked away because she felt the person was more interested in selling her additional products and services than in helping her to lose weight. Anna made the decision to find an independent trainer who only dealt in fitness and nutrition. It is very important to reach out to people who can help us achieve our goals. After researching online, interviewing three different candidates, and contacting referrals from two of them, she was excited to start working with her new personal trainer, Ken.

In their first meeting, Ken asked a lot of questions about Anna's schedule, weight-loss history, and the goal she had. She replied that she wanted to lose weight, increase her energy, and increase her confidence. Ken recommended that she write her goal down. Following the SMART methodology, he helped her to make her weight-loss goal more specific and, therefore, more achievable.

On or before December 31, I want to celebrate having taken control of my health after losing 100 pounds (45 kg) to achieve my goal weight of 140 pounds (63.5 kg). Since it was early February, she felt that this was a realistic goal. However, Ken recommended that Anna cut her goal in half to make it more attainable and realistic. Now it was time for her to step up.

If Anna wanted to keep the weight off, Ken said, she would need to create habits that would be with her for the rest of her life (instead of crash-dieting and then rebounding). Anna could see how she had done the latter many times in the past and agreed to try a "slow and steady" approach. Ken helped her draw up a daily schedule. Anna was sure she would never have made such a detailed plan without his help. Now she could see how positive daily habits and having a plan would lead to long-term success.

The first few weeks of exercise were difficult, but Anna persisted, and the weight started to come off. Then, about two months into the program, she twisted her ankle when she was walking to work. Her first thought was, "Now I won't be able to workout!" She called Ken to cancel. He patiently explained that this was a very common occurrence and they would work through it together. An accident that could have derailed her fitness plan became nothing more than a minor obstacle.

He assured her that he would be there to help keep Anna on track during the inevitable setbacks. Anna had never been taught a system that dealt with setbacks and was happy to hear that her job was to "climb back on the horse" as quickly as possible.

At her monthly weigh-in, Anna found that she had met her goals and could now treat herself to the reward of a new workout outfit—in a smaller size. On her trainer's recommendation, she started to see a nutritionist who taught her to make healthier choices at the grocery store and when she was hungry.

At her September evaluation, Ken congratulated her on a tremendous life change. Her weight was down 35 pounds (16 kg), and, more importantly, Anna had been working out steadily for eight months and had developed some powerful, healthy habits. She had better posture, more energy and self-confidence, and fit into clothes that were three sizes smaller! With the help of her support network, Anna took it one day at a time and made it through the holidays without gaining the usual 10 pounds (4.5 kg). Thrilled, she celebrated New Year's Eve with her friends having lost 46 pounds (21 kg).

Anna succeeded in reaching her weight-loss goal by writing it down, developing an action plan, and finding a support team. The goal gave her the focus she needed to invest in herself, ask for support, and overcome the inevitable obstacles. Anna took her new knowledge and confidence and set some additional weight-loss goals for the next year—keeping them SMART and knowing that she would be able to meet the challenges.

Don and Cindy

Don and Cindy, a couple in their early thirties, had decided it was time to start a family. Both had secure jobs and earned a good living, but they were anxious about their current financial situation and the effect having a child would have on their day-to-day living and financial decisions. In July 2010 they attended one of my financial-planning seminars and, afterward, set up an appointment with me to go over their situation. We evaluated the different goals they had with respect to their finances and their soon-to-be-growing family.

When we looked at their credit card and consumer debt, I knew it was time for a reality check. Cindy had used a student line of credit to help put herself through law school, and Don had student loans as well. Although they had paid the debts down since graduation, they were still sizeable. Not only did Don and Cindy have student debt, but they each had two credit cards that were very close to their limits, as well as loans for their two luxury cars. Their debt came to a total of $120,000, $30,000 of which was on high-interest credit cards.

Even worse, they had no system to keep track of all the bills that came into the house and, as a result, were often late with their payments. When I pulled their credit reports, I saw credit scores that were lower than recommended. I explained that with better credit scores, they would be able to qualify for a better mortgage rate.

It was obvious to me that they were living on credit and that an unexpected "rainy day" would drive them into financial hardship. Certainly, the addition of a baby would bury them unless they developed better spending habits and a system to take control of their finances. When I laid it all out in front of them, they knew it was serious and asked what they could do. I introduced them to creating SMART goals, and this was their first one:

> By June 30, 2012, we will have reduced our credit card debt to zero and our overall debt load to $50,000.

> This met all of the SMART goal criteria because:

> - It was **specific** and **measurable** with dollar figures and a deadline.
> - It was **attainable** and **realistic** given their incomes and determination.
> - It was **timely** because it had a definite due date.

From this overall SMART goal, we were able to create several smaller, monthly goals that would get them to their target. The money they saved during that first month, and in the months that followed, was put directly toward reducing their credit card debt. That first month's goal looked like this: By January 31, 2011, we will eat dinner at home eight times (this month) with food that we prepare ourselves.

As a young corporate lawyer, Cindy was rarely home before nine, and they almost always ate out—a habit that can lead to financial and health issues. Don was able to rediscover his love of cooking because he could focus on making just eight meals a month; the next month they increased the total to 12 meals. They began to take lunch with them to work to save even more money, and each week they reviewed their progress and planned accordingly with the help of their specific goals.

If they had tried to do everything in that first couple of months, they would have set themselves up for failure: proceeding slowly, specifically, and steadily was the key. Don and Cindy were amazed at how much less they were spending with just a few small tweaks to those habits that had had such a direct effect on their financial-planning goals.

Over the next year, they exchanged their luxury cars for a mid-sized sedan, which reduced their monthly payments significantly. They also rose to the challenge and began to examine each purchase they made with a critical eye, no matter how small it seemed. When I pointed out to Dan that his daily cappuccino cost him $1,000 per year, they purchased a cappuccino maker so that Dan could get his caffeine fix at home and put more money toward reducing their debt.

I was relieved to see how well they were doing with taking charge of their debt reduction. Although each change they made was small in itself, the total impact on their spending was huge. As a reward for their hard work, they looked through the real estate listings in their areas of interest. And although Cindy's heart belonged downtown, they knew it made more financial sense to live a bit further away, where their money would buy more house for a growing family. Thanks to great public transit routes, downtown would still be easily accessible.

Although their goal was to pay off their credit card debt by the end of June 2012, they had succeeded in paying off their cards by the end of 2011! The rest of their debt was down by more than 50% by the original deadline.

These improvements to their finances, plus the systems we put in place overall, meant that their credit scores had come up to very good levels. Don and Cindy had learned that specific financial habits were the key to their future success. Importantly, their plan now included a safety net for their new family.

In July 2012, Don and Cindy found a great home for a great price and used part of their savings for a down payment. In September 2012, they became the proud new parents of Cynthia, a beautiful, healthy girl. We still have regular meetings to ensure that they are on track, but the stress that was caused by their finances has now been replaced by the stress of being new parents—a great trade as far as they're concerned.

Chapter Summary

- Dream big and make a list of 50–100 goals you want to achieve.
- Identify when you want to achieve your goals.
- Organize your goals chronologically.
- Do some work to learn the financial implications of those goals.
- While researching your goals, identify any obstacles that need to be addressed for you to achieve them.

How To Eat An Elephant.ca—Web Tools

Goal-Setting Tool

Now that you have an understanding of how to write down your goals, it is time to build your list. Start by logging into www.how toeatanelephant.ca and fill in your profile. When you have completed your profile, you will arrive at the menu page.

Take a minute to read the welcome message and watch the video. When you are ready, click on the **Goal-Setting Tool**. Here you will see the five steps to go through to set up your goals properly as outlined in this chapter. So let's get started!

> **STEP ONE:** Enter a goal in the box provided and click on the **Add** button. Keep repeating this process until you've entered as many goals as you can think of that you wish to achieve. Click on the **Save** button to ensure that they are saved. You always have the option of editing or deleting a goal. Once you are finished entering your goals, click on the **Add Timeline** button.

> **STEP TWO:** Go through each of your goals and enter the time-frame in which you wish to achieve your goals. For example, you may wish to buy a new car in four months. Beside your goal of buying a new car, enter the number "four," and select **Months** from the drop-down list. Do this for each goal and when you are finished click on **Rank My Goals**. You will have the option of ranking your goals alphabetically, by their time frame, cost, or amounts saved.

> **STEP THREE:** Now go back through all your goals, entering how much it will cost to achieve each of them and how much you currently have saved. If you have one large savings account for all your goals, you will need to decide how much to allocate to each of them. If there is no financial cost to your goal (for example, one might be to make your lunch every day) simply enter "$0" as the cost and the amount currently

saved. Once you've done this for all the goals, click on the **Save** button and then click on the **Enter Obstacles** button.

STEP FOUR: This is an optional step where you have the opportunity to list any foreseeable obstacles to achieving each of your goals. If you press the **Add an Obstacle** button beside each goal, a field will appear in which you can enter the obstacle. When you are finished, simply click on the **Save** button and then click on the **Get Report** button.

STEP FIVE: Here you are presented with your report, which you can download and print as a PDF document.

I encourage you to spend some time working with this tool to ensure that you have all of your goals listed. Come back and visit this tool often to update and change your goals as needed. Keep a copy of your goals in a place where you can review them on a daily or weekly basis. Be sure to share a copy of these goals with the people who are important to you, to help keep you accountable for achieving them.

2

WHERE ARE YOU NOW?

A man is lost before he begins if he does not know the ground he stands on.

—*Anonymous*

NOW THAT YOU KNOW WHERE you are trying to get to, you need to understand where you're starting from, and then you will be able to map your course of action from here to there. To do this properly for a financial plan, you need to prepare a net worth statement. This doesn't require a lot of work, just a little bit of organization, a little bit of patience, and a little bit of thought.

Net Worth Statement

A net worth statement is a document that lists all of the assets you have, all of the debts you have, and then subtracts your debts from your assets:

$$\text{Assets} - \text{Debts} = \text{Net Worth}$$

It is important to divide these items into three categories:

- The assets and debts you have
- The assets and debts your spouse has
- The assets and debts you have jointly

There are many reasons for separating them out by ownership, but the biggest reason is for tax planning.

The Canada Revenue Agency (CRA) taxes each person individually. For this reason, financial planners need to know who owns what to be able to show you how to structure your assets to save you taxes. For example, if you are a high-income earner and your spouse is a low-income earner, it is better for you to pay all the household bills and for your spouse to make the investments. This way, any income that is made on the investments is taxed in the hands of the lower-income spouse. This saves the family more tax dollars and increases its overall wealth—rather than that of the government!

Another reason to do this is because some couples keep all their assets and debts separately and run joint accounts for joint expenses. It is important for both spouses to understand where the other stands financially because this can have a significant effect on a couple's ability to reach and achieve common goals. For example, you and your spouse may have a common goal of retiring in 10 years, at age 50, with $80,000 a year in income. One spouse has $400,000 saved and the other has only $10,000 saved. Unfortunately, your goal may be unattainable! It is important for both individuals to understand the other's financial situation.

Here is a simple example of what a net worth statement might look like:

Assets	You	Spouse	Joint	Total
House			$460,000	$460,000
Car	$18,000	$26,000		$44,000
RRSP	$42,000	$38,000		$80,000
Savings			$6,000	$6,000
Furnishings			$40,000	$40,000
Jewellery	$15,000			$15,000
			Total Assets	**$645,000**

Debts	You	Spouse	Joint	Total
Mortgage			$328,000	$328,000
Car Loan	$4,000	$6,000		$10,000
Credit Cards			$5,539	$5,539
Line of Credit	$3,250		$22,000	$25,250
Furniture			$11,000	$11,000
			Total Debts	**$380,189**

Total Assets - Total Debts = Net Worth		**$264,811**

How Do You Figure Out What Assets You Have?

Start by gathering up your financial statements or log on to your investment accounts. Don't worry if you miss one or two—you can always go
back and fill them in later.

Personal Assets: These are assets that you use in your everyday life,
such as: your home, cottage, car, furniture, jewellery, electronics, artwork, and collectibles. Try to be conservative in estimating their worth.
Something you treasure may have a lot of value to you but may not
have the same value in someone else's opinion.

Liquid Assets: These are the investments and savings that you can
quickly and easily convert into physical cash: chequing and savings
accounts, cashable savings bonds, money market mutual funds, etc.
Assets held in a registered retirement savings plan (RRSP) or pension
account cannot be considered liquid assets, because if you tried to
withdraw the money, you would end up having to pay taxes and penalties on the full amount.

Short-Term Investments: These are investments with a short-term
maturity date, such as guaranteed investment certificates (GICs),
Canada Savings Bonds, treasury bills, or the cash value of a life insurance policy.

Equity Investments: Equities are partial ownership in an asset.
Typically, it is ownership in a company or business. For many of us
this includes stocks, preferred shares, mutual funds, pension assets,
and any company stock plans (employee stock-purchase plans, profit-
sharing plans). This is where you would list RRSP equity assets, in
other words, any mutual funds or stocks that are in your RRSP.

Fixed Income Investments: Fixed income is any type of debt owed
to you. Examples include corporate bonds, government of Canada
bonds, and debentures. Within an RRSP, the following are considered
fixed income: GICs, Canada Savings Bonds, and high-interest savings
accounts.

Other Investments: Not all assets fit into one of the categories above.
Maybe you have an investment in a limited partnership, a business

you own, an investment or rental property. Maybe you own a piece of a co-op or time-share. Have you lent a family member or friend some money that should be included as an asset as well? Do you have some Canada Savings Bonds or stock certificates in physical form? Whatever the asset is, get it recorded on your net worth statement. If you are not sure what category it belongs to, simply add it in at the end.

One Frank Thought

If you own stocks on certificate, I highly recommend that you deposit them into a brokerage account. This creates an electronic record of your certificate so that you don't need to worry about the certificate being lost, stolen, damaged, or destroyed in a fire.

Next, I want you to take a look around you and try to determine the value of those assets that you won't find on financial statements. These could include antiques, coins, stamps, comic books, and baseball card collections—anything that could have significant value.

If you're really not sure if something has value or not, one easy trick is to go onto eBay and type in the description of the item to see what a comparable item is selling for online. If you think you have a rare item, chances are one like it is being sold on eBay right now. Remember that just because you think something has value doesn't mean that others will feel the same way. An item is only worth what someone else is willing to pay for it!

Don't worry about ensuring that you have every single one of your possessions listed here. Only the big items are important; many smaller items would sell for a nominal value (if you had to sell them).

How Do You Figure Out What Debts You Have?

It is very important that you list all your debts because they form a very important part of your overall financial plan.

Go through your statements or jump online to get the most recent statements for all of your credit cards. Then get a copy of your most recent mortgage statements showing your mortgage balance, interest rate, and payments. Now gather up any car loan, personal loan, and line of credit information. Do you owe anyone in your family any money? Be sure to list that as well.

Here are the seven pieces of information you need:

- Name of the company you owe the money to
- Type of credit (credit card, line of credit, mortgage, loan)
- Total credit limit on the account
- Total amount owing on the account
- Interest (as a percentage) charged on outstanding amounts
- The minimum monthly payment
- How much you are paying toward each debt

Name of the Company: This is important as it enables you to distinguish among each of your debts.

Type of Credit: It is important to understand what type of credit you have so that you can learn how to optimize your debt repayment by borrowing from lower-cost revolving credit (credit that can be borrowed back once it is paid down—such as a credit card or line of credit). This information is also used in the calculation of interest. For example, you may have a "no money down for 26 months" furniture loan that has no interest, so you aren't in a hurry to pay it down. The problem is that if you don't repay the entire loan by the due date, then you will be charged outrageous interest from the day you bought the product! This can more than double the cost of the product.

Total Credit Limit: It is important to understand how much credit you have available. This helps you to calculate your gross debt-to-service ratio and total debt-to-service ratio (key ratios used by lenders to qualify borrowers).

Total Amount Owing: You need to know this to calculate your net worth and determine how much to pay against your debts and how long it will take to pay them off.

Interest Charged: Some people may be surprised to learn how much interest is charged on their debts. This is critical to understand and determines the calculation of items such as minimum payments, number of payments remaining, and total cost of debt.

Minimum Monthly Payment: This is the minimum amount the borrower has to repay by the due date to avoid being in default. This helps in the calculation of debt repayment and the number of payments that remain.

Payment Toward Each Debt: This is the amount you are currently paying toward the debt each month if you are not paying it off completely.

It is important for you to know and understand what debts you have, the interest being charged, and how much is needed to service your debts. If the total amount of debt surprises you, you may want to go back to your goal-setting and add debt repayment as one of your goals. In Chapter 4 you will learn how to pay off your debt faster and save hundreds of dollars in interest.

Now you can see what your current net worth is: all your assets minus all your debts. This gives you a clear understanding of where you are today financially and will help you to recognize and focus on which goals are important and which ones might have to wait. For some of you, finding out where you are might make achieving some of your goals even easier than you expected. For the rest of us, let's be sure to carry on to the next chapter to learn how we can identify, prioritize, and reduce our expenses in the hope of reaching all our goals and dreams.

Congratulations! This month you've completed the next step in getting your financial affairs in order. I hope it didn't cause you to sweat too much, and you'll come back and continue with the process next month.

Warren and Stella

Six months ago, Warren and Stella appeared to have life totally under control. Still in love after 17 years of marriage, Warren was a partner in a successful accounting practice, while Stella looked after their busy household and volunteered in the community. In their early forties, with two beautiful children, a large home, and two new cars, their life was a model of success.

Warren worked long hours at his office. He was normally out of the home by 7 a.m. and often not back until after 8 p.m. During tax season, he regularly worked six or seven days a week and rarely saw the kids. Each year, this was a stressful time for their family, and each summer they took a major family vacation to make up for it.

Stella was heavily involved on volunteer committees at a women's shelter and active at her children's school. Their 3,600-square-foot home required a significant amount of her time to maintain, and Stella liked to keep it spotless, even with two young children. They also entertained friends and clients on a regular basis. Stella usually took responsibility for planning these events.

Warren played pickup hockey with his friends at the local rink every Saturday during the winter. In the heart of tax season, March, there were not quite as many players as usual and, as one of the younger guys, Warren found himself playing back-to-back shifts throughout the game.

When he started to feel chest pain toward the end of the game, he knew he had played too hard. By the time he had taken his equipment off, the pain was radiating throughout his left side. Even though he knew the symptoms of a heart attack, he couldn't believe it was happening to him, a "young guy," so he tried to drive home. Halfway there, he fell unconscious and crashed into a ditch. Another motorist called 911, and an ambulance arrived. After resuscitation efforts, he was taken to the hospital. When Stella received the call from the police, she called her parents to ask her mom to look after the kids, and had her dad drive her to the hospital. She waited with Warren for the rest of the night, praying that he would be okay.

Warren did survive, barely, and during his prolonged recovery in the hospital, Stella suddenly found herself in charge of everything, including the family's finances—a task that had always been Warren's responsibility. She didn't know what to do with the bills that began coming in. She didn't even know where the family's papers were kept—the wills, power of attorney documents, personal care directives, and critical illness and life insurance policies that she needed to act on behalf of her husband and family.

Luckily, Warren had organized these papers and prepared for an emergency, so they were kept at their lawyer's office. Stella obtained the documents she needed and began to apply for his critical illness insurance, a process she had never imagined she would be doing one day. She realized how lucky she was that Warren had purchased this insurance.

In the past, Warren had written Stella a cheque each week to take care of the household expenses. She had no access to the other accounts because they were not joint accounts. With power of attorney, Stella was able to access the accounts from which the bills were paid. It was then that she realized she had no funds left to pay the mortgage at the beginning of April.

This was the first of a number of unexpected discoveries. Stella found out that their house had a second mortgage, in the form of a line of credit, that Warren had been using to support his business (which was not doing as well as she had thought). She was embarrassed that she didn't even remember signing the papers for it. Warren asked for her signature on a regular basis, and as she trusted Warren completely, she never even thought to ask what she was signing. Not only that, but Warren's credit cards were maxed out and their two new cars were in negative equity due to depreciation. Her single credit card had a $1,000 limit that she meticulously paid off in full each month from the money that Warren gave her. She definitely was not ready for this financial situation.

Luckily, the insurance company was quick to pay out on the critical illness policy, and this allowed her to pay the bills and mortgage until Warren was back at work. When he recovered, Stella had a serious conversation with him about their finances, and they came to see me as a couple. Stella is now an active partner in their financial matters: their accounts are jointly held, and she knows exactly where all their important papers are kept.

Warren and Stella's net worth statement:

Assets	Stella	Warren	Joint	Total
House			$732,000	$732,000
Car	$38,000	$47,000		$85,000
RRSP	$34,956	$137,000		$171,956
Savings	$2,000			$2,000
Furnishings			$45,000	$45,000
Jewellery	$20,000			$20,000
			Total Assets	**$1,055,956**

Debts	Stella	Warren	Joint	Total
Mortgage			$522,000	$522,000
Car Loan	$45,000	$53,000		$98,000
Credit Cards		$30,000		$30,000
Line of Credit			$100,000	$100,000
Furniture			$5,000	$5,000
			Total Debts	**$755,000**

Total Assets - Total Debts = Net Worth			**$300,956**

Bob and Susanne

Bob and Susanne are a lovely couple in their early fifties. Bob is a senior manager at a chemical company and has worked there for his entire career since graduating from university with a degree in chemical engineering. Susanne has been an executive assistant for the past 12 years, working her way back into the labour force after raising their two children, Tom and Chris.

Bob and Susanne came to see me after Bob was unexpectedly handed an early retirement package by his company. Although they have consistently contributed to their RRSPs, and Bob has a company pension, they weren't expecting retirement quite so soon and wanted to ensure that they would be okay financially.

At the end of our first meeting, I gave them the net worth worksheet and sent them home to gather their documents. Although they were skeptical about being able to prepare a net worth statement, I assured them it wasn't that difficult and told them to make a date out of it!

After they arrived home, Bob and Susanne looked at each other and started laughing nervously: the situation seemed so hopeless that it was laughable. The problem was that, although both of them had been steadily employed, they had never really been on top of their finances. They had an approximate idea of where their money was, but they had no clue how it was doing or where the paperwork was. It seemed clear to the couple that the process of completing their first net worth state-ment would be a bit of a challenge, but it didn't have to be painful. They took my advice literally, and, on their first financial "date," Bob poured a glass of wine for each of them while Stella put on their favourite music — show tunes! — and they gathered around the dreaded filing cabinet. The poor thing was bursting with papers. The drawers barely shut and bits of paper peeked out around the edges. Beside the filing cabinet was a box stuffed with more papers, and on top of the box was a pile of unopened envelopes containing financial statements and reports. After the crash in 2008, Bob had simply stopped opening their state-ments, figuring it was better not to worry about long-term investments.

Susanne brought a garbage can and a recycling bin into the room. On my advice, they had also purchased a small shredder to get rid of any documents that contained their personal information but were old enough that they were no longer important. Any statements older than 10 years went into the to-be-shredded pile. That first night, they worked for two hours, opening envelopes, sorting statements and bills into file folders, and setting up a system to deal with the paperwork.

On their next financial date, Bob and Susanne were able to make real progress in their sorting. They had separate sections of the filing cabinet set aside for insurance policies, RRSPs, Bob's pension, bank accounts, their mortgage, and everything else they needed to com-plete the net worth statement.

The third financial date was used to complete the sheet. At our next meeting, they were eager to share what they had found. Bob laughed (in a good way) as he told me that they were actually excited to finally be getting on top of their finances, that they had set a date for the next night, and that Susanne had started during the day to help out even more.

After reviewing their net worth and preparing a comprehensive financial plan, it looks like they'll be just fine. In fact, they'll be more than fine, they'll be great! After half a lifetime of working hard and living within their means—albeit in an unorganized and cluttered way—Bob and Susanne have amassed sufficient savings and can now look forward to a comfortable retirement. This kind of knowledge and peace of mind was only possible because they made financial "dates" to get on top of their finances.

Bob and Susanne's net worth statement:

Assets	Susanne	Bob	Joint	Total
House			$458,000	$458,000
Car	$14,000	$10,000		$24,000
RRSP	$293,488	$381,691		$675,179
Savings	$10,000	$8,000		$18,000
Pension		$632,173		$632,173
Furnishings			$7,000	$7,000
Jewellery	$15,000			$15,000
			Total Assets	**$1,829,352**

Debts	Susanne	Bob	Joint	Total
Mortgage			$52,000	$52,000
Car Loan	$2,000			$2,000
Credit Cards	$1,500	$1,200		$2,700
			Total Debts	**$56,700**

Total Assets - Total Debts = Net Worth	**$1,772,652**

Chapter Summary

- Know where you are now to get to where you want to be (goals).
- Make a list of assets in each person's name.
- Gather up all statements.
- Don't forget about real assets (house, car, cottage, etc.).
- Make a list of debts.
- Determine interest rates, minimum payments, etc.
- Remember to include any loans to or from family and friends.

How To Eat An Elephant.ca—Web Tools

Net Worth Tool

This tool will help you organize all your assets and debts in one place to see exactly where you stand. Start by gathering documentation pertaining to all your assets and debts.

> **STEP ONE:** Log into www.howtoeatanelephant.ca and select the **Net Worth Tool** from the menu.
>
> **STEP TWO:** Begin entering each asset by selecting the category that it would belong to followed by the type of asset. Then enter a description the owner, and the value of the asset. Click on the **Add** button and repeat this process until all of your assets are entered. At any time you can edit or delete an asset, and when you're finished entering them, click on the **Enter Debts** button.
>
> **STEP THREE:** Enter each of your debts by categorizing the owner of the debt. Give a name to the debt to help you identify which one it is, and then select the type of debt from the drop-down list. Now enter the outstanding balance, the minimum monthly payment, the monthly amount you're paying, the interest rate charged, and the maximum credit limit available on this debt. Then click on the **Add** button. Once you have completed entering all your debts, click on the **Save** button and then click on the **Get Report** button.
>
> **STEP FOUR:** Here you are presented with your report, which you can download and print as a PDF document.

It may seem that you have entered a lot of information that is not relevant to your net worth, but this will help to save you substantial time and effort when you use other tools.

It is important to understand who owns the assets and who owns the debts to be able to develop a tax and financial plan that effectively saves you money.

3

HOW TO SAVE A LOT OF MONEY!

It's better to look ahead and prepare than to look back and regret.
—*Jackie Joyner-Kersee*

IN CHAPTER 1, WE DREAMED ABOUT where we wanted to get to (our goals). In Chapter 2, we identified where we are today (our net worth). In this chapter, we're going to look at what resources we have to help us get from where we are today to where we want to be. The process of identifying what we have to enable us to reach our destination occurs when we prepare a budget. Yes: the "B" word!

What Is a Budget?

A budget is a record or projection of all the money coming into the house and all the money going out of the house. It is also known as a cash-flow statement. This term makes it easier to visualize: money flows in and money flows out. Unfortunately, more money tends to flow out.

Why Is a Budget Important?

A budget is *paramount* to financial success!

You need to know how much money you have and what it is being spent on to be able to prioritize spending and allocate funds toward different goals. Whether the goal is retirement, travelling, buying a new car/house/boat, the kids' education, paying off credit card debt, or even a wedding, you need to understand where you will get the money from to pay for these things.

The hardest part of the process is to figure out the answer to: "Where am I spending all my money?" You may have a mortgage or rent a house. You likely have to pay utilities, such as water, heat, electricity, cable, internet, phone, cellphone, maintenance fees, condo fees, or property taxes. If you own a car, you may have to cover a lease or loan payments, car insurance, maintenance, fuel, parking, and registration fees. On top of that, you likely have family needs, such as food, clothing, visits to the hair salon or barber, daycare, and transit passes or tokens. You may also have activity expenses for swimming, dance, piano lessons, babysitters, or a tutor. These are just some of the essentials you need to be able to live and function in our society.

Now let's look at some of the more flexible expenses that may or may not apply. Some of these optional expenses may be vacations, gifts for your family and friends, and entertainment. Entertainment can include going out for dinner, going to a movie, seeing a play, watching a live football game or some other sporting event. Also, what about magazines, newspapers, and subscriptions to online services, or satellite radio? Don't forget donations to charities and religious organizations. These are all part of your household expenses. What about all those once-a-year expenses as well? Items such as memberships to clubs and gyms. Sometimes insurance policies are renewed annually, too.

And, finally, let's not leave out paying our debts: credit card bills, lines of credit, and personal loans to family and friends. All this . . . and we haven't even started saving money!

What about Pocket Money?

This tends to be one area where a lot of people lose a lot of money to things they can't identify. Some people spend up to $7,000 a year, before taxes, on minor expenses, such as coffee and lunch.

One Frank Thought

If buying coffee and lunch every day is one of your goals, and a priority, then I don't have a problem with that, but for the majority of people I've met, purchasing coffee and lunch every day is pretty low on their priority lists.

Here's how the math works:

- Morning coffee and muffin: $4.50
- Mid-morning coffee: $1.50
- Not-so-healthy lunch: $8.00
- 3 p.m. pick-me-up (chocolate bar, pop, or donut): $1.25
- Rotten groceries/leftovers thrown out of the fridge: $2.75

Add it up and in one day *you have spent $18!*

That's $90 a week on coffee and bad food! If two of you are doing it, add another $15 to the daily total, and the weekly spending comes to $165! To top it all off—and we all do this—there will be at least one night during the week that you'll order in, take out, or eat out. At a minimum, this is going to cost you $20. Your weekly total is now $110, or $205 for a couple or family. This $110 equals $5,500 a year in after-tax dollars (50 work weeks with two weeks for holidays) or $7,100 of your salary. Wow!

Needless to say, the list of expenses can get very long and very tedious, so it is important to ensure that we identify where all the money is going.

One Frank Thought

If this book does nothing else but teach you how to build a proper budget and manage that budget efficiently, then you will have benefited tremendously.

There are two ways to figure out where all of your pocket money is going:

1. Old School (but still very effective): Every time you purchase something, ask for a receipt. Keep all the receipts in an envelope, and every day/week/month, tally them up. Start by sorting them into groups of expenses, such as coffee/lunch/snacks, parking, magazines, and miscellaneous. This will help you determine how much money you spend and where you typically spend it.

2. New Age: Get the app! Most smart phones have a budget application available for download. Applications that I have used and tested are iExpense and Spenz for the iPhone®. They are very simple to use, and it takes less time to enter the expense than it does for the clerk to give you your change! I'm sure there will be many more applications available by the time this book is published.

One Frank Thought

Like most things, these apps are only good if they are used consistently. So use them! It will open your eyes to a whole new awareness of how much you spend!

Where Have I Spent My Money?

There is absolutely no reason to fear preparing a budget.

There are a number of reasons why people are reluctant to budget. Some are afraid that it is a lot of work or they don't really know how to do it. Those who have tried have never been able to keep to it (likely because they were doing it wrong).

Yes! It does require some work. Fortunately, with today's technology, it is getting easier and easier. Websites such as www.mint.com, software programs such as Microsoft Money or Quicken, and many of Canada's big banks have good tools you can use. You can also download all of your account and credit card transactions to another application on your computer or smart phone.

One Frank Thought

Double-check your expenses and budget categories. Sometimes purchases do not get categorized properly when you are using software, and items may be counted when you don't want them to be counted. Be sure to go through your statements line by line to ensure that they are correct.

How Do You Get Started?

1. To prepare a good (accurate) budget, you (and your partner) need to set aside four to five hours.
2. Gather up at least the last three months' worth (12 months is better) of bank and credit card statements. (Including the credit cards your spouse does not know about!)
3. Use the **Expenses Tool** found on the website www.howtoeatan elephant.ca as a guide to identify the various categories of expenses. It is important to understand how much you spend on various items so you can identify where you may be overspending and then cut back.
4. Start going through all your statements line by line, noting the category that each item belongs to.
5. Start filling in the spreadsheet to determine how much you spend every month.

Once you have entered all your expenses, take a look at the total and ask yourself this:

"I spend how much?!"

There Must Be Some Mistake!

When they have built their budget, many people are surprised by the large amount of money they spend every month. This may be due to the fact that they are not calculating their budget properly. Before you freak out, let's review it to make sure you haven't missed anything or made a miscalculation.

Mistake #1—Not Everything Is Paid or Charged on a Monthly Basis

This is a common error. If you pay $500 biweekly for your mortgage, you don't pay $1,000 a month. You actually pay $1,083.33 a month! This is because there are approximately 4.3 weeks in a month and not a perfect 4. Your hydro bill comes every two months, so if you didn't account for it in your monthly budget, you will be short. If you did account for it, but included the entire amount in that month, your budget will show you spending more than you really are.

Solution

Identify how often something is paid, either to or by you. Take a look at the last three bills you received. They will usually indicate the period of time they cover. For example, a cellphone bill may say it covers usage from February 20 to March 19. Therefore, it is a monthly bill. Your water bill may say it covers water usage from March 21 to June 30, which is 104 days. I think it would be safe to count this one as billed once every three months.

Once you have identified the frequency of the bill, apply the following formulas to determine the monthly budget amount:

- Weekly = $ amount × 52 /12
- Biweekly = $ amount × 26 /12
- Monthly = $ amount
- Bimonthly = $ amount × 6 /12
- Quarterly = $ amount × 4 /12
- Semi-annual = $ amount × 2 /12
- Annual = $ amount /12

For example, if your water bill is $135 and it is paid quarterly (every three months), multiply $135 × 4 = $540 and then divide this by 12 = $45. Therefore, you include $45 in your monthly budget.

Mistake #2—Not All Paycheque Deductions Are Equal

We will look more closely at income in the next chapter, but an area where many people make mistakes is in recording the deductions from their paycheques. The most common error comes from miscalculating deductions for Employment Insurance (EI) and the Canada Pension Plan (CPP). Both max out at a certain point in the year (depending on your income). Therefore, if you used paycheques from the first part of the year to determine the deductions taken in a full year, you may be deducting too much.

Also, some people have benefits that come off one paycheque, but not another, and some have union dues that are paid once a month, or annual deductibles for insurance benefits.

Solution

Take three or four consecutive pay stubs and try to determine a pattern. Check the Canada Revenue Agency's website for the CPP and EI maximum premiums as calculated against income. At the time of writing, the 2012 premium amounts are a maximum $2,306.70 for CPP on $50,100 of income and a maximum $839.97 for EI on the first $45,900 of income. For the self-employed, the maximum premium for CPP is $4,613.40.

Mistake #3—Double Counting

This happens when people have money taken off their paycheques for a pension, RRSP, or other savings accounts. When they fill out their budget, they list it twice because it's on their mind. Another example of this mistake is when you include eating out or ordering in under "entertainment" and also under "food" (i.e., groceries).

Solution

Be sure to categorize each expense only once as you go through your credit card and bank statements. Do not start filling in the budget spreadsheet until you have done so. If there isn't a category for a specific item, create one for it. It is really important to be patient and diligent when preparing this document.

Mistake #4—Not Including Everything

Without going through a full year's worth of statements, it is very easy to miss or forget about some items—especially those that you pay only once a year. Maybe it is an annual dividend, or an association membership, or professional dues, or an insurance premium. Whatever these expenses are, if you miss them, they can really throw a budget out of whack before you even start to get things under control.

Solution

Build an annual payment section into your budget. This may include things like memberships, dues, insurance premiums, magazine/newspaper/website subscriptions, car registration, and kids' school fees. After you have grouped them all together, take the total and divide it by 12 to add it to your monthly budget.

Money Is Finite!

One of the biggest keys to financial success is understanding that money is finite. If you start to live by this principle, then you quickly learn that spending a dollar over here means that you don't have that dollar to spend on something over there. Children, especially teenagers, struggle to understand this principle because they just go to the "Bank of Mom and Dad." It becomes critical to your financial success to identify where your money is being spent, prioritize where you want it to be spent, reduce your necessary expenses, and eliminate spending on superficial wants.

Now that you've dug through your expenses and found them all, let's understand what is a *need* vs. what is a *want*.

Needs vs. Wants

In the economic boom of 2006, Victoria's Secret launch a bold advertising campaign with the glitzy statement: "Give me everything I WANT, and nothing I NEED!" It punctuated what I believe is one of the biggest issues in our society today and is a great example of why so many of us are in financial distress. As a society we are so focused on obtaining and having everything we want that we are finding it difficult to meet basic needs— especially to safeguard our future.

I want you to take a few minutes to review your goals list. Which ones are the most important? You've already identified when you want to achieve these goals, so now it's a matter of finding the resources to go out and do it. Keep these goals in your mind as you work through the next exercise. I want you to ask yourself constantly:

> Do I want to spend my money on this expense, or do I want to put it toward one of my goals?

One Frank Thought

Work with your partner and/or an objective person in your life; it really helps to make you more accountable. Be honest with yourself and ask: "Would my life be fundamentally affected without this expense?" Remember to keep asking yourself that question: "Do I want this expense more than that trip to Hawaii?" If you are frustrated and fed up with your debts, the need to pay them off may override your want for new clothes, shoes, or golf clubs. If you're really unsure if a particular item is a want or a need, then just put a question mark beside it and come back and revisit it later.

Breaking the Spending Habit

Many people have spent the better part of their lives trying to manage their money in one way or another. When you finally decide to take the initiative and get a handle on your finances, one of the hardest things to do is to break the spending habit. If you've been a dedicated consumer and have racked up a lot of consumer debt—mainly in the form of credit cards or lines of credit—take those credit cards and bank cards and put them away. By forcing yourself to pay for everything with cash, you will realize quickly how much you are spending.

It is also a psychological thing: it is much harder to count out $140 in cash to pay for a new outfit than it is to hand over a piece of plastic. Casinos understand the psychology all too well. This is why they never allow you to play with cash. It is much easier to place two or three colourful chips down on a table than it is to lay down $300 in bills!

One Frank Thought

I came to this realization one time while playing blackjack at a casino. I was winning a little bit and was feeling good, and I increased my betting to $50 a hand. A short while later I was dealt a hand that allowed me to add to my bet by splitting pairs and doubling down. Before I realized what I was doing, I had wagered $300 on one hand! If I had to take out $300 in $20 bills to make the same bet, I would have hesitated and thought about it each time. Because they were only poker chips, I didn't feel like I was wagering all that much. The same is true of credit cards: when all you do is put down a plastic card, you really don't get a sense of how much you are spending.

Put Yourself on a Cash Diet!

Look at your personal budget and how much you want to spend on discretionary items, such as coffee, lunch, candy bars, snacks, magazines, and that special shirt that's on sale.

Let's say you budget $40 a week for your discretionary spending. Although that doesn't sound like that much to some, it adds up to more than $2,000 a year.

Here's what I want you to do every week: on Monday morning, put the $40 in your purse or pocket. That is all the money you have to spend until the following Monday. This forces you to think about whether or not you want to buy something. So, if by Wednesday afternoon you've already spent your $40, you no longer have any money to spend on discretionary items. On Thursday morning, if you want a coffee, you'll have to bring it from home because you don't have $2.75 to spend.

When it comes to spending your other budgeted money on items like clothing or gifts, ask yourself: "Is this a want or is this a need?" If it's a want, ask yourself the question: "Which do I want more, this item or that trip to Hawaii?" If the answer is the trip to Hawaii, put the item back.

If it is a need (and be honest about that), then ask yourself: "Does it have value? Could I get this same or a similar item somewhere else at a lower price? Do I need it right now? Could I wait for it to go on sale?" The answers to these questions will determine whether or not you purchase that item.

One Frank Thought

Everything goes on sale eventually. Typically, stores need to turn over their inventory once every three to six months. You can also always ask if they will sell it to you at a lower price. Hey! If you don't ask, you don't get.

Here is a great flow chart that explains how to make up your mind if something is a want or a need.

The Guide to Shopping Discipline

Nice item! → Is it a WANT or a NEED? — WANT → Do you want it more than a goal? — No → Put it back!

NEED? ← YES

Does it have VALUE? — NO → Put it back and wait for SALE

YES ↓

Go ahead and buy it

The 10% Rule for Financial Success

You've likely heard this advice many times before: Save 10% of what you earn, and you can achieve financial success. David Chilton made the idea famous in his book *The Wealthy Barber*. Throughout my years as a financial planner, I have heard repeatedly the excuse that people don't have money left over to contribute that 10%. So here's how you're going to find your 10% and possibly much more.

Go through all of the expenses you haven't eliminated—both the needs and the wants—and find a way to shave off a modest 10%.

If you are like the average Canadian family, you likely spend close to $5,000 a month on all of your expenses. By putting in the effort to find ways to reduce your monthly expenses by 10%, you could find $500 or more a month, or $6,000 a year, to put toward your goals.

Now, I can already hear many of you saying, "Wow! That would be great, but there's no way I could do that." So here are a few things to consider doing to achieve this 10% reduction:

- Call your utility and service providers and ask them to find a way to reduce your costs by at least 10%. In many cases, there are alternative solutions that can still meet your needs at a reduced cost. If you don't ask, you don't get!
- If you're planning a family outing, start by going online and doing a search to see if there are any two-for-one coupons, or other deals. Even if it will only save you $10, remember: money is finite. If you spend it over here, then you won't have it to spend on your other goals and dreams.
- Plan ahead, make your lunch and take it to work every day. Doing this alone could save you $5,000 or more a year.
- If you have a fair amount of debt, be sure to read the next section of the book to learn how to substantially reduce that debt and save a lot of money and interest charges.
- If you find it difficult to exercise restraint in the holiday season, and you're spending a small fortune on gifts, have a serious conversation with your family about wants vs. needs and have them participate in identifying which is more important. Do they want the latest video game or a family trip to Hawaii? Consider developing a secret Santa or similar gift-giving strategy to reduce spending.
- If you have a mortgage, speak with your mortgage lender to see if there's a way to reduce your interest rate.
- When it comes to your utilities—heat, electricity, and water usage—work together as a family to change habits and reduce consumption.
- Home phone, cellphone, internet, and cable can be bundled together to reduce your expenses tremendously. Call your providers and

ask them to work with you to find a way to reduce these expenses based on your habits. When thinking about cable, ask yourself how important it is to have the super-duper sports and movie packages and all the extra channels when you really don't watch them or watch them only occasionally. Ask yourself, "Do I want to have these cable channels more than I want to accomplish my goals?"

- When dining out, start by looking online to see if there is a coupon available. Also, check with your credit card company to see if they have a discount if you use your card at a specific restaurant.
- If you hire domestic help, such as a house-cleaning service or a dog walker, see if you can have them come less frequently to save you some money. Spend an extra 10–20 minutes a day walking the dog or cleaning the house.
- Start a neighbourhood borrowing club. Speak with your neighbours about what books, magazines, DVDs, video games, board games, and so on they may have that you can borrow. Just be sure when you are lending them out that you keep track of who's borrowed them and if they've been returned.
- If you have a gym membership, use it or lose it! If you can't get out of the contract, go to the gym and get yourself in shape and spend that time feeling better about yourself. Being healthier will also help you save money on over-the-counter and prescription drugs because you may no longer need them.
- If you have life insurance policies that have a cash value built up within them, you may be able to take a premium holiday. Contact your insurance broker to learn more about this.
- If you need equipment for your children to play sports, put the word out to all your friends and family to find out if anybody has anything the kids can use. Most sports equipment is barely used and there is a ton of it available.
- Having a baby? Congratulations! When sharing the news, ask if anybody has any gently used items that would help as you care for your child.
- Do you donate money to charity? Although it does generate a tax deduction, you might consider donating your time instead. This is

also a great way to network and connect with like-minded people in your community.

- Clothing? Open up your closet and start digging through it. You will be amazed at the number of clothes you've forgotten you own. Also, talk with friends and family who are about the same size as you and arrange to exchange clothing with them. For some people this can shave hundreds of dollars a month off expenses.
- Gifts for friends and family? By planning ahead, you can likely find on sale the gifts you want to give.

Additional Tips for Reducing Expenses

Here are four ways you can save up to 40% on your grocery bill:

1. Start by making a meal plan. Studies have shown that people spend 18% more on their grocery bill by randomly walking around the grocery store picking items off the shelf.
2. Use grocery store flyers to build your meal plan around the food that is on sale that week. So if chicken breasts, cheese, and tortillas are all on sale, consider adding quesadillas or fajitas to the meal plan.
3. Don't shop at high-end grocery stores. Sixty per cent of your groceries will come in the form of packaged goods. These can be purchased at a discount grocery store for 10% less.
4. Go shopping in your pantry. Many households have between $100 and $300 of groceries sitting in their kitchen cupboards. If you use up $15–$20 a week of those groceries, this can start to really add up in savings.

How I Saved $1,154 After-Tax Dollars with Two Phone Calls

Call up each of your utility and insurance providers and explain to them that you can no longer afford the services and see if there is anything they can do about reducing the costs. If they are unwilling to work with you to reduce the costs and find less expensive alternatives, then spend a few minutes online to find somebody who will.

I called my cable TV and internet provider recently and did exactly this. With hardly any hesitation, they were willing to offer me a deal that would see my internet service costs reduced by 25% and my cable TV bill cut in half! This will end up saving me more than $500 a year. So after that call, I decided I would call my cellphone provider to find out whether or not they could do something similar. My cellphone provider reduced my cellphone bill by nearly 40%, saving me close to another $500 a year.

You can save from 20 to 40% or more on gifts for family and friends by planning ahead and shopping throughout the year. If you see something you think would make a great gift and it is on sale, purchase it (even months) in advance of giving it to them. You can save on vacations too if you spend some time looking for a great deal or work with a good travel agent.

If you're planning on eating out one day of the week, try takeout instead. This will not only save you the 15-to-20% gratuity you typically leave, but you will also save by providing your own beverages rather than purchasing the high-priced drinks you get at restaurants.

Do you ever have a pizza night? Rather than ordering a pizza that can cost you $20 or more, try one of the new frozen pizzas that are now available. These can cost you as little as $4 if you watch and buy them on sale. Even if you need two or three of these, it is still a substantial saving.

Now that we know where we are spending our money and have learned a few tricks and tips to help us save money, we can start allocating that money toward our goals. Remember, money is finite. If we spend it on things that aren't important to us or not part of our goals, we won't have the money to help us achieve our goals.

Cathy

A couple of years ago, Cathy felt a financial pinch when her employer let her go. This was the first time in her adult life that she had found herself unexpectedly unemployed, and although the jobless period lasted for only a couple of months, it had been incredibly tough. Her savings had disappeared within a couple of weeks (admittedly they hadn't been very substantial), and she had lived off her credit cards for two months until her new paycheque started.

After her hiatus, she had thrown herself into work, buying the new wardrobe she needed for her new, more professional workplace, as well as working longer hours. She glanced at her bills and made her minimum payments but didn't really think about her finances in detail until the day she received an invitation to her 10-year high school reunion. She suddenly realized that she didn't have the money to buy the plane ticket to get back home or to pay for a hotel room. Or money for a killer dress.

At our first meeting, Cathy told me about the Friday night she sat in the middle of her living room with bills all around her and reality set in. She was living from paycheque to paycheque and barely making her credit card and student loan payments.

Being stuck in this situation also got her thinking about what she wanted to accomplish in the next few years. She had always wanted to travel. As she stared at her bank statements, she realized that if she continued living this way, she would never have the money she needed to take those trips. She was sure she was making enough money, but couldn't understand where it was it all going.

I spent some time showing Cathy the power of preparing a budget and identifying and distinguishing between wants and needs. Cathy had always avoided budgeting, but she decided to give it a try. I gave her a great spreadsheet, similar to the one at www. howtoeatanelephant.ca, and helped her work through it. Since she had never kept close track of her finances, it took a bit of coaching to get her to assemble all the paperwork, including RRSP contributions and monthly bills. We also included the unexpected expenses that we rarely think about or plan for but that seem to occur on a regular basis, like a high school reunion or car repair. Cathy wanted to make sure her budget was as accurate as possible and showed great perseverance in entering the previous year's expenses. She brought the spreadsheet with these figures to our next session and we went through it to find areas where she could save and areas where she wanted to invest to achieve her goals. We also discussed why a budget is useless without a goals list to show where you want to be and why.

In Cathy's case, there were a couple of areas where infrequent but significant expenses were jeopardizing her financial stability. As we went through her budget, she wasn't sure if she could cut back or eliminate some of these expenses. I got her to think about her goals and what was more important to her. This really made a difference, and she started slashing her budget left, right, and centre.

One of the biggest areas of concern was gift-giving. Cathy does not have any children herself, but with four older brothers and sisters and a total of nine nieces and nephews under the age of 12, she has taken upon herself the role of "cool auntie," which means gifts for birthdays and holidays and lots of meals and movies out. Cathy loves giving, but it wasn't until she looked at her budget that she realized her annual expenses for family gifts were close to $3,500. When she added in the gifts she purchased for her friends, it was closer to $4,500. Cathy was floored: she had had no idea that the occasional $30 to $70 gifts she loved to buy were such a significant expense. We brainstormed ways that Cathy could show her love for her family and friends while reducing the overall cost of her generosity. By preparing special craft days for her nieces and nephews and carefully buying gifts on sale throughout the year, Cathy agreed that she could cut her gift-buying budget in half, and maybe more.

She also realized that she was spending more than $5,000 a year on coffee and lunch. She started taking lunch to work and kept a few dinners in the freezer to cover those nights when she was working late and didn't have time to prepare a meal. By making a few changes she figured she could easily save $3,000 a year. She decided that she wasn't going to give up her weekly lunch out with co-workers and the every-now-and-then fancy coffee that she loved.

By taking these steps to control her spending, and using the budget to free up funds to pay down her debt and save for short- and long-term goals, Cathy no longer dreads life's unexpected occasions. She now feels that she is controlling her money instead of her money controlling her!

Derek and Linda

Derek is a father of three and a computer analyst for one of the big banks in Toronto. He is fanatical about having a budget and sticking to it—something that the rest of his family resents. In fact, Derek and his wife, Linda, came to see me because financial issues were slowly tearing their marriage apart, and their marriage counsellor knew some expert financial advice would help.

Derek felt that Linda was not mindful of the family's expenses, always demanding that they go on family vacations, have elaborate parties, new clothes, and, well, the list went on. Linda, predictably, felt that Derek was cheap. They had agreed that she would stay at home with their three boys to save on daycare and house-cleaning expenses. Indeed, when they had done the math on daycare for the three boys, the monthly expenses had turned out to be almost the same as Linda's after-tax salary as an assistant store manager for a national chain. Financially, it had made sense for Linda to stay home.

What Linda hadn't anticipated was the feeling of powerlessness that would come with having no income. She told me how, every week, she had to ask Derek for money to run the household and to then justify every expenditure to him for his budget reconciliation. If she decided to have coffee with a friend, she would hear about it from Derek and receive a lecture on how tight they were financially.

These situations are delicate, but not uncommon. Single-income families have built-in power imbalances that often lead to trouble. This trouble often ends up in the family courts, but I was fairly sure that I could help Derek and Linda with their issues.

They both had valid points—it is disempowering to have to ask for money, and money was tight. Even though Derek made a very good salary, between deductions for savings, taxes, and benefits, there never seemed to be enough left. And with three boys under 10, there were many expenses to deal with. All three boys played soccer, and the eldest also played indoor soccer in the winter. The two younger boys played house league hockey as well. Linda and Derek wanted to keep their kids active and involved.

Although Derek tracked their expenses carefully, he had no idea how to use the budget to gain control of their finances. He was simply tracking their slow descent into debt and becoming more and more anxious. This translated into abruptness and anger when dealing with Linda's weekly requirements.

Using Derek's spreadsheet, we began to divide each line into fixed and optional expenses, needs and wants. After examining their budget, we identified some major line items that were really impacting their budget. Derek had a membership at a golf club that he never used and that also had a minimum monthly food-and-beverage charge. Another item was parking fees that Linda paid for convenience when running errands. Yet another was pocket money. Although they could attribute the pocket money to lunch and takeout for the kids, they were surprised this was adding up to nearly $300 a week. Combined with the parking and golf membership, they were spending nearly $2,300 a month! I spoke with both of them about the fact that money is finite. If you choose to spend it on things like eating out and club memberships, you don't have it to spend on vacations and other things that might be more of a priority.

Both Linda and Derek were reluctant to change their spending habits until I showed them that by going on a cash diet and cancelling the unused membership they would free up more than $13,000 each year. This was more than enough to pay for an annual vacation and to build an emergency account. Both Derek and Linda lit up when they saw this number.

This is what I mean by the freeing power of budgets. They are not scary; they are just numbers, but the numbers give you the power to plan your life so that you get the most out of the financial resources you have.

Once they saw how saving on fixed items could move them toward their goals, they attacked their budget with gusto. They called their service providers and made new deals for the phones and cable, as well as their furnace-maintenance package. Then they got even more serious and renegotiated their mortgage. It was a year early, but low rates more than made up for the penalty they paid. In fact, they were able to change their payments to biweekly and are now moving toward their goal of being mortgage-free faster than before.

I also made sure that Derek understood it was essential for Linda to feel empowered financially in their relationship. To that end, they prepared a household budget and arranged to have the appropriate amount transferred from Derek's account to Linda's account every two weeks. Linda then took on the responsibility of keeping track of her part of the family budget. Instead of the weekly or daily arguments they had been having, they now reconcile their books once a month as financial partners as well as life partners.

About a year after we first met, I saw Derek and Linda again to see how things were going. They told me about all the things they were now saving money on and about the great vacation they took with the boys at Disney World. They also shared the story about their adult escape to Jamaica, which Derek found at a great sale price. They were completely different people than the couple that sat in front of me a year ago—more relaxed and confident, smiling instead of scowling. Derek also made sure to point out a line item in their budget that they were able to cut out last month: marriage counselling!

Chapter Summary

- Identify where all your money is being spent.
- Gather up three or more months' worth of credit card and bank statements.
- Categorize your spending.
- Identify wants vs. needs.
- Cut out wants and change spending habits.
- Cut spending on needs by 10%.
- Focus on your goals and priorities.

How To Eat An Elephant.ca—Web Tools

Expenses Tool

Start by organizing all your bank and credit card statements as well as any cash receipts you may have. Once you are in this tool you will notice there is a monthly cost calculator to help you determine how much you should enter for a given item each month. As you read earlier in this chapter, some expenses are paid more than once a month and some are paid less than once a month. This calculator will help you to determine how much to include in the **Expenses Tool**.

> **STEP ONE:** Log into www.howtoeatanelephant.ca and select the **Expenses Tool** from the menu page.
>
> **STEP TWO:** Start by selecting the category and enter the monthly amount you are paying for each of the items. Now identify whether each expense is a **Need** or a **Want**, or indicate you are **Unsure**.
>
> **STEP THREE:** When you reach the **Debts Category,** you will see that it has been pre-populated with the debts that you entered into your **Net Worth Tool.** You will need to enter how much you pay on a monthly basis on each of these debts and determine which ones represent a **Need** or a **Want**, or indicate you are **Unsure**.
>
> **STEP FOUR:** When you have completed entering all your monthly expenses, you can click on the **Save** button and then click on the **Get Report** button.
>
> **STEP FIVE:** Here you are presented with your report, which you can download and print as a PDF document.

Spend some time using this tool and ensure that you have done it correctly. Knowing exactly where and how your money is being spent empowers you to make decisions that can greatly affect your quality of life. Identifying each expense as either a need or a want will help you to find additional funds that you can put toward goals that are a greater priority. Once you have completed this tool, go back through the report and see if you can identify where you can reduce your expenses by at least 10%.

4

INCOME AND DEBT MANAGEMENT

The man who never has money enough to pay his debts has too much of something else.

—James Lendall Basford

NOW THAT YOU KNOW WHERE your money is being spent, we need to track down where you are getting the money to pay for everything.

The most obvious source is a paycheque. But to truly understand how much we bring home, we need to identify a few things. First of all, how often do you get paid? Some people are paid weekly, others are paid biweekly. Some people are paid twice a month and many more are paid monthly. There are a few who are paid quarterly, but they are the exception rather than the rule.

If you are paid weekly or biweekly, you need to understand that you don't receive four paycheques a month (weekly) or two paycheques a month (biweekly). You actually get paid 4.33 or 2.16 times a month. Why is this significant? When you are preparing a budget, you need to know that every third or sixth month you will end up with an extra paycheque! This can make an enormous difference in your ability to meet your budget or accomplish your goals. Most often, people don't realize that they are actually missing out on 8% of their income. In many cases, if you took this 8% and put it away for retirement, you could meet your retirement goals.

Let's look at the example of Marianna, who earns $52,000 a year (or $1,000 per week). If she budgets only $4,000 a month in income, she will have an extra $4,000 left over at the end of the year:

$$\$52{,}000 - (\$4{,}000 \times 12)$$

If she took that $4,000 every year for 25 years and invested it, achieving an average 7% return, she could end up with nearly $253,000 saved!

What other ways can you increase your income to meet your budget and reach your goals? Well, if saving for retirement, education, or buying your first home is a priority, put money into your RRSP directly through a payroll deduction. When the money is taken off your paycheque directly, it isn't subject to income tax. Using the previous example, if Marianna directed $77 a week from her paycheque to her RRSP, her paycheque would decrease by only $52. After 25 years, she would have saved about $271,500. The reason her pay will only decrease by $52 and not $77 is because she does not have to pay tax on the $77 going directly into her RRSP. Now Marianna is meeting her retirement-savings goal and still has an additional $25 per paycheque more than she budgeted for. This adds up to $1,300 a year. Maybe this is enough for that vacation she's always wanted?

Another action you can take is to ask your HR department for the TD1 form for the next tax year. You fill this out in December. The TD1 form is a Canada Revenue Agency form that allows you to list all the deductions you will have in the coming year, such as education courses, or expenses related to a dependent child, spouse, or parent. Maybe you are a caregiver, or over the age of 65, or will be using your dependent tuition credits. These options reduce the amount of tax deducted from your paycheque and increase the amount of income you have to cover your expenses. You have to fill out the TD1 form every year. If you don't, your employer won't know that you have these deductions, and will continue to take tax off your pay at a higher rate.

Other areas in which you may be able to find some income are through a rental property you own; renting a room; housing an international student; dividends, interest, or capital gains on investments; yard sales; selling collectibles on eBay; or working at an occasional cash job. Don't forget to include income from spousal and child support, pensions and any regular gifts you receive.

Income that many leave out of their records is bonus or incentive pay. Make a conservative estimate of your anticipated bonus and divide it by 12 to include it in your monthly budget. We will examine how taxation affects these various sources of income in Chapter 10.

Debt Destruction

Another way to increase your cash flow is to pay down and pay out your debt. When you "optimize" your debts, what you are doing is borrowing money from the lowest-interest debt to pay out the highest-interest debt. This ensures that you will pay the least amount of interest possible (without doing a consolidation loan). This will help you to pay out your debt faster because more money will go to the principal rather than the interest.

So let's say you had two credit cards (VISA and The Bay) and a line of credit with a balance owing on all three items. The interest on the VISA credit card is 18.95%, on The Bay it's 26.95%, and the line of credit charges 8%. Borrow all the money available on the line of credit to pay out all the credit cards (or as much as you can). This will reduce the interest you pay and more money can be applied against the principal of the debt, ensuring that you pay it out sooner. By making the minimum monthly payments on all your debt and then taking the rest of the money and paying it against the highest-interest debt first, you will reduce your interest costs substantially and be debt-free sooner.

The goal is to pay out the highest-interest debt first, then, once that debt is paid off, you can apply the full payment from that debt to the next-highest-interest debt along with its minimum payment. This accelerates the payment of the next debt, and it will be paid off quickly. Then you "snowball" that payment into the next debt item, and so on, until all the debts are gone. You will be amazed at how quickly and easily you can get all of your debts paid off.

Example:

	Interest Rate	Balance	Limit
The Bay	26.95%	$2,500	$3,000
VISA	18.95%	$2,000	-$2,500
Line of Credit	8.00%	$4,000	$5,000

Step 1: Borrow the $1,000 of available credit from line of credit and pay down The Bay card.

Step 2: Borrow the $500 of available credit from the VISA and pay down The Bay card. Now your Bay card has $1,000 left owing the VISA is maxed out owing $2,500 and the line of credit is maxed out owing $5,000.

Step 3: Make the minimum payments on the VISA and line of credit and use all extra money to pay down The Bay card until it is paid off.

Step 4: Once The Bay card is paid off, take all the money you were paying to it, add in the minimum payment you were making to the VISA and pay down the VISA as quickly as possible while still making the minimum payment to the line of credit.

Step 5: Continue with this format until all your debts are paid off.

Now, this is a very effective and proven strategy to destroy your debt quickly, but it won't work if you don't have your spending under control. If you are paying down your debt and running up charges on another credit card simultaneously, you will find yourself in a never-ending cycle.

Debt Consolidation

Debt consolidation is another way you can pay off high-interest debt and reduce the number of payments you need to make overall. A loan or line of credit is used to pay out your other, higher-interest debts. For example, you can borrow money at 8% and pay out your higher-interest debt, like credit cards with 18% or 26% interest rates. This allows you to have fewer debts to repay and manage. You need to qualify for the credit, which could pose a challenge if you have been mismanaging your debts. You may also need to learn how to live without credit cards, which might be a good thing. Again, this will work to reduce and eliminate your debt only if you have your spending under control and are not racking up debt elsewhere.

A word of caution about debt consolidation: this can be the first step down the road to bankruptcy. If you do not get a handle on your over-spending, you can end up maxing out on your debt and being forced into bankruptcy through what is known as debt pyramiding.

Debt Pyramiding

Debt pyramiding develops when you consolidate your debts with a consolidation loan, which frees up the credit available to you, and then you go out and rack up more debt and get another consolidation loan. This frees up a little bit more credit—which you then max out and, eventually, you are forced into bankruptcy.

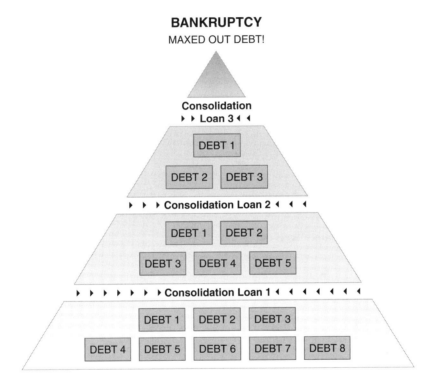

BANKRUPTCY
MAXED OUT DEBT!

**Consolidation
▸ ▸ Loan 3 ◂ ◂**

DEBT 1

DEBT 2   DEBT 3

▸ ▸ ▸ Consolidation Loan 2 ◂ ◂ ◂

DEBT 1   DEBT 2

DEBT 3   DEBT 4   DEBT 5

▸ ▸ ▸ ▸ ▸ ▸ ▸ Consolidation Loan 1 ◂ ◂ ◂ ◂ ◂ ◂ ◂ ◂

DEBT 1   DEBT 2   DEBT 3

DEBT 4   DEBT 5   DEBT 6   DEBT 7   DEBT 8

Breaking the Cycle

To truly get ahead, you need to break the cycle of purchasing things on credit and then paying them off over time with interest. If you can get the debt paid off and start saving up to purchase the item, you will save a lot of money in interest charges.

A fundamental change in your current behaviour needs to happen before you can break this cycle. You first need to make the decision once and for all that you are going to control the money rather than let the money control you! Until this happens, you will not break the cycle. For some this will be much harder than for others, and some may even need to seek counselling. I want you to start by recognizing that you don't *need* most of the things you are currently spending your money on. Once you see that it is just stuff that is creating this pile of debt and leading to your increasing levels of stress and anxiety, you will quickly be able to change your mindset and focus on the things that really matter.

Credit Counselling

If you are finding that you are getting buried in bills and your stress and anxiety are becoming overwhelming, you may be wise to contact a local credit-counselling agency. These agencies are typically not-for-profit and will work with you to get a handle on your budget and debts. After reviewing your entire situation, they will show you how you may be able to stop the interest charges and pay out your debt once and for all. They will help you to understand which repayment option is best for your situation.

Debt Management Program

This is a program where you work to repay all your creditors and all your debts over a 48-month period or less. The credit counsellor will work with you to get your creditors to stop or substantially reduce your interest expenses and set up a monthly repayment plan. During this time, your creditors will rate your debt on your credit report as being in collections (R9). Once you have repaid the debt in the 48 months, your creditors will upgrade your debt to (R7) for another two years. The debt management program is not a legal process. It is a voluntary process.

Bankruptcy and Insolvency Act Options

These options require that a consumer debtor be legally insolvent (i.e. the value of all your debt is more than the value of all your assets).

Consumer Proposal

This is a legal route through which a proposal for repayment is put to all of your creditors. If creditors representing 50% of your debt accept the proposal, then all of your creditors must abide by the proposal. The 50% is based on the dollar value of your outstanding debt. For example: Let's say you have the following debts:

$36,000 to Visa
$48,000 to MasterCard
$88,000 to TD line of credit
$42,000 to BMW Canada

Your total debts are $214,000. The debt owed to TD and BMW is greater than 50% of the total debt outstanding. So if TD and BMW accept your creditor proposal, then Visa and MasterCard will be forced to accept it, too.

The consumer proposal arrangement means that creditors accept a percentage of the total debt to be paid in monthly payments over a period of time, usually 48 months, as payment in full. There is no interest in a consumer proposal, and it allows you to keep your assets. Again, you will have to make regular monthly payments for 48 months, and you will have a collection (R9) rating on these debts during the 48 months and for three years following the repayment.

Bankruptcy

This is the last option. It may be required that most of your assets be sold (liquidated) to repay the debts through a trustee in bankruptcy. Or, you may have to pay the equivalent value of the asset to compensate for the asset's value. You will have your income garnished to repay the debts. Half of any surplus income (as calculated by the courts) will be payable for 9 to 21 months to your creditors. You will have this record of bankruptcy on your credit report for eight years.

Contact the counsellors in your area or reach out to those at Credit Canada (www.creditcanada.com, toll-free 1–800–267–2272) to learn more about which option is best for you.

Debt Service Ratios

When determining the amount available to you for your mortgage, lenders will use two common debt service ratios.

Gross Debt Service Ratio (GDS)

When calculating GDS, the lender considers your monthly mortgage payments, heating costs, condo fees (if applicable), and property taxes. They will also include any repayments to your home buyers' plan (if applicable). The rule of thumb is that your monthly housing costs must not exceed 32% of your gross family income.

Total Debt Service Ratio (TDS)

When calculating TDS, the lender considers all the expenses in the GDS calculation, plus payments to credit cards, lines of credit, and bills, such as phone, cable TV, etc. This time the rule is that all of your monthly costs must not exceed 40% of your gross family income.

Good Debt vs. Bad Debt

Not all debt is bad. If you use debt to improve your financial net worth, this is considered good debt. Examples would be borrowing to purchase a home rather than paying rent, purchasing a rental property that generates income, and purchasing income-producing investments. Other forms of good debt include student loans so that you can complete a degree or diploma, or a loan to start a new business that generates income for you.

When debt is used to purchase a depreciating asset, it is only compounding the loss of value. For example, using credit to buy a car, consumer goods, such as an iPad®, cellphones, computers, a TV, or furniture, or to pay for vacations or to eat out, reduces your net worth and financial well-being.

Mortgages

A mortgage is most likely the largest debt you will ever incur in your lifetime, so it is important that you understand how it works and the best way to structure it.

How Much Can You Afford?

The amount of money you can afford to borrow for your mortgage is only one part of the equation. When you purchase a property for the first time, or if you are trading up to a larger property, there are always additional expenses. People often forget to consider or include expenses such as property taxes, maintenance, moving expenses, legal bills, land transfer fees, and, of course, the need to buy new furniture and redecorate. Other costs may include appraisals, home inspections, renovations, refinancing penalties, and other soft costs you haven't thought about.

If you determine that you can afford a mortgage payment of $1,400 a month according to your budget, and you haven't factored in all these other payments, you may want to look at a mortgage payment of about $1,000. This will ensure that you have enough money left over to cover all the other expenses.

One Frank Thought

We have been in a very low-interest mortgage environment for many years now. Rates are still at their lowest level in more than 60 years (at the time of writing this book). Many analysts predict that mortgage rates will increase significantly in the coming years. Although I agree that rates will become higher over time, I believe it will be at a modest pace. That being said, I recommend that people calculate their mortgage payment based on a rate that is 60% higher than the current five-year rate and see if they can still afford their mortgage payment.

At the time of writing, the five-year rate was 3.19%, so if you calculate your mortgage amount with an interest rate of 5.10%, it will help you to weather any major increases in mortgage rates in the near future. Remember: how much mortgage you can qualify for is not necessarily how much you can afford!

What to Consider When Getting a Mortgage

Questions to ask yourself include:

- How long do I plan to own this property?
- Is the mortgage portable (i.e., can you move the mortgage to a new house)? This is important if your mortgage rate is really low

and a few years down the road the rates are much higher and you want to move.

- What are my payment and prepayment options?
- Can I write off the interest as a tax deduction?

Payment Options
The Power of Prepayments!

Having the flexibility to make additional payments against your mortgage is paramount to you saving substantial money on interest charges. Many lenders will allow you to prepay against the principal up to 15% of the original amount borrowed, in addition to letting you increase your regular mortgage payment by up to 15% of the current payment. On top of that, they will let you do this each year!

Although you may never intend to use it, it is a good idea to negotiate as high a prepayment option as possible (some lenders will go as high as 30% of the original mortgage amount). The reason for doing this is to give you greater flexibility (and a lower mortgage interest penalty to break the mortgage) should you decide to move the mortgage to another lender or pay it out entirely. Typically, a mortgage penalty will be based on the balance owing after the maximum prepayment has been applied, so it is important to negotiate this option.

Fixed vs. Variable Rate

The choice between fixed or variable rate mortgages has sparked one of the biggest ongoing debates among providers of financial services. (Another, newer debate is about whether to contribute to an RRSP or a Tax-Free Savings Account. Look for the answer to that one later on in the book.)

The simple answer to this question? A variable rate has been proven to be a better choice than a fixed-rate mortgage in both rising and falling interest-rate environments. This option saves you more money. So why do so many people purchase five-year fixed-rate mortgages?

1. They like the security of the guaranteed fixed payment for five years.
2. People who sell mortgages encourage you to purchase a five-year mortgage because they make more money from the sale of it.

If you do decide to choose a variable-rate mortgage, set your payments in your budget based on a higher rate. Use any excess money you have from that payment to help pay for (potentially) higher payments down the road.

What to Consider When Renewing

Always negotiate the best possible rate available in the market. If the lender isn't willing to give it to you, another lender will, and they will be happy to cover the cost to move your mortgage. Be sure to revisit your budget and see if you can afford to increase your payment, make a prepayment, and/or shorten the amortization period for your mortgage.

Leslie and Stan

Leslie and Stan are in their mid-forties. They have two daughters who are currently studying at university. One studies visual arts, and the other studies engineering. About a year and a half ago, Leslie's grandmother passed away, and Leslie received an inheritance of almost $100,000 when the estate was settled. After much discussion, Leslie and Stan used the money to pay off their credit cards and to pay down the line of credit on their house.

They had also agreed to take $10,000 of the inheritance and, along with their daughters, use it to take a three-week, once-in-a-lifetime trip to Spain last summer. It had seemed like a good idea at the time, but about six months ago, Leslie started to have second thoughts. Where had the money gone? Well, she knew where it had gone: to pay down their credit cards and the line of credit. But now she was watching the balance on their credit cards creep back up, and she was starting to panic.

She didn't want her inheritance to have been for nothing. She and Stan came to see me, and the first thing I had them do was figure out how much they were spending. I asked them if this was the first time in their lives that their credit-card spending had caused problems. Sheepishly, they admitted that, no, they had carried balances for most of their married lives and that since the girls had gone to university, they had been relying on credit cards more and more to make it to the end of each month. It wasn't that their income was low. On the contrary, Leslie and Stan were successful and their income was stable, but the money just seemed to slip through their fingers.

After we looked at their cash flow—the money coming in and going out—I had to agree with them that, yes, there simply wasn't enough money for them to do it all. It's a pretty common problem. I explained that money is finite: if you spend it in one area, then it won't be there to spend in another. We began to look at ways they could reduce their spending, especially while the girls were in school. One of the possibilities was to roll their creeping credit card balances onto their home line of credit. But that would only work if they didn't started spending their balances back up immediately—which they were likely to do, based on their history.

I asked them the hard question: what were they willing to sacrifice to become financially sound? Their answer was equally hard: nothing. They liked the lifestyle they had. Leslie enjoyed taking lots of self-development courses and travelling. Stan is a huge lover of classical music, and he wasn't willing to give up their season's tickets.

We reached an impasse, and I laid it on the line. They were on their way to wasting the inheritance and running their debt levels right back up unless they took some meaningful action to make their expenses match their income. They went away to think about their goals.

Two weeks later, Stan and Leslie came back for another meeting. They told me that it had been a couple of busy weeks, and they were ready to try again. Their eldest daughter had decided to take her master's degree, and they were now looking at several more years of tuition. In addition, Leslie's older brother had had a mild heart attack and, although he was recovering, they were rather shaken and thinking seriously about their life goals.

Now we were able to get down to work! Sadly, it often takes a crisis to persuade people to really start thinking about their goals and life plans. After a lot of discussion, we hit upon a creative solution to their financial problems. With the girls away at university, their home was feeling empty. It was a fairly large home, close to transit and a university campus in Wolfville, Nova Scotia, so we agreed that they could create an income suite in their basement. The renovations could be financed through their home line of credit, with the space created when they'd used the inheritance to pay it down. The completely separate and legal suite would, when rented, increase their cash flow by at least $1,000 per month. This would cover their mortgage payments and, with some moderate spending changes, they would have the cash flow they needed to maintain their priorities—education, travel, and the arts—while staying financially secure.

Stan and Leslie are now in their second year of being landlords and love it. Combining an increased income with the reduction of some of their expenses and a forced saving plan is helping them to live the quality of life they wanted without running up the debt. They keep their goals in mind as they develop their budget each year and have not encountered any further trouble with credit cards, paying them off in full each month.

When Stan and Leslie went into the bank to discuss a loan to help pay for their daughter's master's degree, they were pleased to learn that they not only qualified, but at a preferred rate due to their improved credit rating!

Tom and Julia

Julia and Tom are a couple with big goals. Both are in their early thirties; Julia is a family doctor, and Tom works in the IT department of a mid-sized company. Together, their income is close to $175,000 a year, and when they contacted me a year ago, they were planning to start their family as soon as possible. There was only one big problem: the house.

One of their biggest goals, and the first step on their way to starting a family, was to buy their dream home. Purchased in 2007, when mortgage rules were at their most relaxed, they had paid 5% down on a 40-year mortgage at an interest rate of less than 4%. It had seemed like the perfect deal. They had been approved, due to their low debt levels, good credit rating, and high income, for a $600,000 mortgage. They had found a 3,000-square-foot home that they loved in a new subdivision on the outskirts of Calgary. They had been enjoying their new home, which felt like a palace compared to their cramped downtown apartment.

Things have changed since 2007. When they contacted me, they knew they needed help, but they weren't sure what had happened or what their situation now was. They had been struggling more and more each month to make their mortgage payment, which was just over $3,000, and they had been using credit cards to make up the difference. Even though their careers were progressing well and seemed secure, they were feeling the financial crunch, and they knew that their mortgage was coming up for renewal in a couple of years. With the ever-tightening mortgage regulations, they were concerned that they were going to have trouble qualifying for a new mortgage at a favourable rate.

I asked them when they had last looked at their credit report. Their response was that they hadn't checked since they got the mortgage. I suggested they get updated credit reports to make sure that their credit scores were still high enough to qualify for the best rate. I was concerned about the amount of debt they were carrying on their credit cards. None of the cards had a very high balance on its own, but they had six cards between them, and almost all were close to or at their limit, totalling almost $40,000 of debt. They hadn't really worried about it, knowing that they could make the minimum payments, but I explained that this practice of sitting at the limit could, and would, hurt their overall score.

They went home to put together their budget and waited for the credit scores to arrive. When we met two weeks later, they were ready to get serious. Their budget clearly showed that they were falling short on a monthly basis and slowly slipping deeper into debt. Not only that, but their credit scores had dropped significantly since they bought their home, and their total debt service ratio was quite high. Even with their high incomes, their debt payments were more than 35% of their gross income. How were we going to handle this? Could they reduce their spending enough to make it work?

After a lot of discussion, Tom and Julia made the hard decision to downsize their home, which had appreciated in value over the last few years along with the rest of the Calgary housing market. They sold it for a profit and were able to put 20% down on a smaller home in a more established neighbourhood. This move cut their mortgage payments almost in half and ensured that even if interest rates went up significantly, they would still be able to make their payments. They arranged their mortgage through the same lender and got the best rate possible.

While Tom and Julia were investigating a new home, we worked on destroying their debt. Using the Optimize feature of the Debt Destruction Calculator at www.howtoeatanelephant.ca, we were able to organize their credit card debt and begin to pay it down. With a couple of changes in their spending habits, including Tom commuting on transit and Julia reorganizing her medical office by partnering with other practitioners, the debt and anxiety levels started to drop quickly. Once this was accomplished, they could move ahead on their other plans.

The move had given them more cash flow to pay down their debt, and they used the Debt Destruction Calculator at regular intervals to keep them motivated. With less stress, they were able to enjoy more time together.

It has been a year since we reorganized their finances, and this year at their check-up I was thrilled to see that they are expecting their first child. Time to talk to them about insurance—but that is for another chapter!

Chapter Summary

- Identify where your income is coming from.
- Determine the true monthly amount based on payment frequency.
- Have RRSP/pension contributions deducted at source.
- Request and fill out a TD1 form to reduce your tax withholding.
- Optimize your debt by paying out high-interest debt with low-interest debt.
- Consider debt consolidation or credit counselling.
- With a mortgage, borrow less than you can afford.
- Consider a variable-rate mortgage.

How To Eat An Elephant.ca—Web Tools

Income Sources

This tool will be used to determine your total household income from all sources. Have at least three pay stubs, invoices, or receipts of income ready before using this tool.

> **STEP ONE:** Log into www.howtoeatanelephant.ca and select the **Income Sources Tool** from the menu page.
>
> **STEP TWO:** Start by selecting the number of jobs that you have.
>
> **STEP THREE:** For each job, answer questions one, two, and three, and confirm how much you expect to be paid from each job by answering the question with a yes or no.
>
> **STEP FOUR:** Once you have completed this task for all of your jobs, select all the **Other Sources** of income you may have. Be sure to select all that apply.
>
> **STEP FIVE:** For each additional source of income, enter the annual amount.
>
> **STEP SIX:** After you have completed steps Two through Five for yourself, proceed to doing them for your spouse, if necessary. When you are satisfied that you have entered all sources of income for both you and your spouse, click the **Get Report** button.
>
> **STEP SEVEN:** Here you are presented with your report, which you can download and print as a PDF document.

This report will show you the total amount of EI and CPP premiums you will have to pay as well as approximately how much income tax you will pay for the year. This information is used to determine your marginal tax rate, which is used in future tools.

Now that you know how much money you have coming in, let's figure out how quickly you can pay off your debt!

How To Eat An Elephant.ca—Web Tools

Debt Destruction Calculator

This calculator is used to help you to organize and pay out your debts quickly and effectively to save you hundreds, and possibly thousands, of dollars in interest and have you debt-free sooner than you ever thought possible.

The information in this tool is pre-populated from the information you provided in the Net Worth and Expenses Tools. If you have not completed these tools, please go back and complete them first. Be sure to have current statements from all of your outstanding debts at hand when using this calculator.

> **STEP ONE**: Log into www.howtoeatanelephant.ca and select the **Debt Destruction Calculator** from the menu page.
>
> **STEP TWO**: Review, edit, correct, and total all the debts in the calculator.
>
> **STEP THREE:** When you are satisfied that all the information is correct, click on the **Save** button. If you wish to exclude your mortgage from the debt destruction calculation, select the box beside **Exclude My Mortgage** or else simply click on the **Optimize My Debt** button.
>
> **STEP FOUR**: Read through the explanation of what has been done to optimize your debt and, if you agree with the optimization, click on the **Destroy My Debt** button. Otherwise, select **Undo Optimization**. If you have chosen not to optimize your debt, you will now see your un-optimized debt and you can click on the **Destroy My Debt** button.
>
> **STEP FIVE**: Here you are presented with your report, which you can download and print as a PDF document. You also have the option of seeing how much faster your debt could be paid off and how much additional interest you can save by paying more each month toward your debts. Simply

enter the additional amount of money you believe you will be able to pay toward your debt and click on the **Recalculate** button.

This tool can be a very powerful and effective guide to helping you pay down and pay out your debt and save you a considerable amount of interest. A word of caution: this is effective only if you have your spending under control. If all you are doing is running up other debts while trying to pay out the debt you already have, you're just going in a circle and not getting anywhere. Get your spending under control first, and then aggressively reduce your debt.

PART
TWO

PROTECTING YOUR FINANCES

Managing the Bumps along the Way

5

BENEFITS

To make our way, we must have firm resolve, persistence, tenacity. We must gear ourselves to work hard all the way. We can never let up.

—Ralph Bunche

CONGRATULATIONS ON MAKING IT THROUGH the first four chapters! The work you have completed in these previous chapters has created the foundation for your personal financial success. It has also been the hardest part of getting your financial affairs in order. From here on in it will only get easier, so stick with it, and I promise you will see great results.

The time, effort, and information you have put in so far will be used over and over again as we move forward to give you greater insight, comfort, and confidence with your finances. This will make it easier to get the answers you need to accomplish all your goals!

Group Benefits

Many of us work for a business that offers its employees benefits. The more common types of benefits are health, dental, and prescription drug benefits, often with paramedical, eye care, and long-term disability.

Other types of benefits that are gaining in popularity are flex-benefit plans and healthcare spending accounts (HSAs). Some businesses offer additional benefits to their employees, including child care, fitness-club memberships, low-interest or interest-free loans, and retirement funding or education assistance. Wellness programs that include financial planning, nutrition, fitness, health, and mental well-being are also becoming more and more popular as businesses recognize their value. Many of these are considered taxable benefits.

How Can You Get the Most from Your Benefits?

1. Locate a copy of your most recent benefits coverage booklet. These often are available through your Human Resources department, on your company's internal website, or on your benefit provider's website.

2. Take an hour to meticulously go through the various benefits that are offered to you and consider if they apply to your situation.

3. Make a list of those benefits you expect or need to use and store it in a handy place. (Maybe enter them in a journal or notes section of your email account, or type them up in an email and send it to yourself so you can search for it easily.)

4. Compare your coverage with that provided by your spouse's employer. If you both have coverage, assess how you can get 100% coverage on all things for both of you and see where one has coverage and the other doesn't. See if it makes sense to have family coverage on both benefit plans or, if one plan covers everyone, opt out of family coverage for the other, or opt out of the benefits entirely. Finding optimal coverage in your benefits plan could save you a couple of hundred dollars a year in benefit expenses.

5. Discuss your coverage with your providers, such as your dentist, eye doctor/optician, physiotherapist, etc. so they understand what coverage you have and can do their best to work within that coverage.

6. *Use and claim your benefits!* This sounds silly, but many people can't be bothered to file a claim. Add this to your monthly to-do list or do it right away. If you are going to the dentist and you know you will have to submit a claim, bring the form with you to the dentist and have the receptionist help you fill it out. At the end of your visit, ask them to

print a duplicate receipt for you. This ensures it gets done, and you have someone helping you who knows what information is required. Many systems are now automated, so all you have to do is remember to have your benefits card with you.

7. If you are not sure if something is covered, ask for help. Speak with someone in HR, or call or email the benefit provider directly to learn if there is coverage or assistance for specific items. Many companies provide benefits to their employees through employee assistance providers (EAPs). These third-party providers offer a variety of programs to help employees deal with personal issues. Use the toll-free numbers provided and ask about their services or request a summary of services.

8. *Get the free money!* Many businesses offer employees retirement savings contributions through a matching program. Matching funds or direct funds may also be available for educational and tuition assistance, as well as discounts on health and fitness incentives through training and gym memberships. These can all improve your quality of life, reduce your monthly expenses, and save you from having to come up with the additional money to pay for them. Many of these items are considered taxable benefits when provided by your employer.

Traditional vs. Flex-Benefit vs. Healthcare Spending Accounts

These are three of the most common types of plans on the market. It is important to identify which type of plan you have and how to use it effectively to maximize the types of benefits and money you have available.

Traditional Plans

These plans usually cover many areas of your life and health. Every member of the plan has access to each of these areas of coverage, regardless of whether he or she uses them or not. Typical plans cover short- and long-term disability (see Chapter 6), hospital coverage, travel medical coverage, prescription drugs, dental, eyeglasses and eye examinations, and paramedical services (chiropractic, physiotherapy, psychotherapy, massage therapy, and speech therapy). Other coverage may include term life insurance (see Chapter 7), and many other types of coverage can be added to the plan.

Although these plans tend to be the most comprehensive, they also tend to be the most expensive for the employer.

Flex-Benefit Plans

These plans are what their name says they are: flexible. Typically, the employer chooses a dollar amount that each employee can use to spend on a variety of different benefits. Most of these benefits are similar to the ones offered in traditional plans.

Although there is a dollar amount that is given to each employee, the employer may allow the employee to use some of that money to contribute to stock-purchase plans, tax-free savings accounts, or RRSPs, or simply to be paid out as a taxable benefit.

Other purposes for which the money could be used include purchasing additional long-term disability coverage or life insurance. To maximize your benefit for this type of plan, sit down and review all of the different options with your family to see what types of coverage are most appropriate for your needs. Look back at what you have spent in various areas, such as dental, drugs, and eyeglasses, and talk about what upcoming needs may arise.

One Frank Thought

"Flexibility" means you can change your level of coverage and/or what type of coverage you have. With a flexible plan you may also have an opportunity to negotiate for higher dollar coverage during salary and bonus negotiations, because there are dollar amounts individually set aside for each employee.

Healthcare Spending Accounts (HSAs)

Although healthcare spending accounts have been around for a number of years, many consider this kind of plan to be the new kid on the block.

In some instances healthcare spending accounts are offered in addition to a traditional or flex-benefit plan.

An HSA can be thought of as a benefits bank account that is set up for each individual employee and is funded by the employer. The employee can make withdrawals from the bank account to pay for various types of medical expenses, such as hospital care, dental care, eyeglasses, eye exams, massage therapy, and many others.

Maybe you have a spouse who has a traditional group benefits plan, and it only covers 80% of drug benefits. You could use your healthcare spending account to pay not only for the additional 20% of the cost of the drugs but also for the dispensing fee at the drug store as well. There are limitations on what you can use the money for because, as the title states, it is meant for healthcare spending. The biggest benefit of these types of plans is that you can choose how much or how little you spend on any qualifying healthcare products or services you need.

Unlike the flex-benefits plan, you do not have to choose one of the flex-benefit plan options. The disadvantage is that the funds cannot be used as contributions toward stock-purchase plans or RRSP or TFSA contributions.

Self-Employed/No Work Benefits Options

If you are self-employed, or find that you have no work benefits coverage, start by looking into groups you may already be a part of to see if they offer group benefits (alumni, professional associations, or other groups). You may decide to purchase benefits on your own. There are several options to choose from, including traditional plans—such as the one Blue Cross offers—and flex-benefit options, such as the one Manulife offers.

One point to recognize when it comes to benefits plans is that—aside from catastrophic coverage protection or coverage for long-term disability or term-life coverage—all the benefits essentially are dollars-in dollars-out (minus administration and profit fees for the insurance companies). So if you find you are without coverage and you are thinking about purchasing a benefits plan for dental, drugs, paramedical, eyeglasses, etc., you may be better off negotiating with the individual vendors to find the best and lowest cost alternatives. These plans really have value through their catastrophic protection. So if you end up in a serious accident, a benefits plan helps to pay a lot of your out-of-pocket costs.

If you are a small business and incorporated, you may want to use the affordability and flexibility of a healthcare spending account.

Taxable Benefits

Not all benefits you receive are tax-free. If your economic situation is improved through a benefit, it is usually considered a taxable benefit. (There are a few exceptions, as noted in the Non-Taxable Benefits section below.)

A taxable benefit is a benefit (cash or non-cash) you receive from your employer. If you receive a benefit that is personal in nature, it is a taxable benefit. A benefit can include:

- A reimbursement of personal expenses
- Free use of property, goods, or services owned by your employer
- An allowance

A taxable benefit may be paid in cash, such as a meal allowance or reimbursement of personal cellphone charges, or provided in a manner other than cash, such as a parking space, gym membership, or a gift.

Items considered taxable benefits include:

- Automobile and motor vehicle
- Lodging
- Cellphones
- Child care
- Discounts on merchandise
- Education/tuition allowances
- Interest-free or low-rate loans
- Meals
- Parking
- Tax-free savings account contributions

These are just a few of the more common types of taxable benefits. Be sure to speak with a tax accountant or check with the Canada Revenue Agency for a complete list. For many people, the cost of the taxable benefit is categorized as additional income or other income on their T4 slip.

Automobile and Motor Vehicle Benefits

If you get to use a company vehicle for purposes other than business, it comes under the category of personal use and is considered a taxable benefit.

Personal Driving

Personal driving is defined as driving for purposes not related to employment. This includes travel between home and work.

It is not considered personal driving if you travel from your home to a point of call (a place other than your office or place of business), such as visiting a customer site or returning home from that site. If this applies to you, try to schedule all your meetings outside the office at the beginning and at the end of your day.

Non-Taxable Benefits

There are a few benefits that are paid or given to employees that are not taxable. Examples of these include:

- Counselling services
- Professional membership fees
- Health benefits
- Use of the company's recreational facilities
- Uniforms and other special clothing
- Gifts under $100

If you are unsure as to whether or not something is a taxable benefit, consult your HR department or check with the Canada Revenue Agency.

Employee Assistance Programs (EAPs)

Many benefit plans also include employee assistance programs. As the title states, these programs are designed to assist employees with a variety of different counselling and educational services. Provided by third parties and kept confidential, these services are typically free or are substantially subsidized for the employee.

Be sure to contact your HR department to learn if you have an employee assistance program as part of your benefits and gather some information on what services it provides. Some of the common types of services offered are:

- Emotional and mental health
- Relationships and family
- Workplace concerns
- Work–life balance and stress
- Addictions
- Physical health and nutrition
- Career questions
- Child and eldercare
- Legal and financial concerns

Leave of Absence

There may be a time when you need to take a leave of absence from your work. With some benefit plans, you may lose the benefits entirely during that time away, or you may have an option to pay for the cost of maintaining your benefits during your leave of absence. In many cases, it may make sense to pay the fees to maintain your benefits while on leave to ensure you can continue to use them.

Travel Medical Insurance Coverage

Many people are not aware that their group benefits plan provides travel medical insurance coverage, and they go out and buy third-party or additional coverage when it's not necessary. Be sure to take the time to check if you have this coverage through your group benefits plan and review it to ensure that it is appropriate coverage. Some travel insurance will not cover you for certain activities or when travelling to certain places and countries.

If you are unsure, do not hesitate to call the insurer to have all of your questions answered. It is always better to be safe than sorry. There are many instances when people have fallen ill or been seriously injured while on vacation and their provincial medical coverage barely covers any of the costs. The last thing you want is to go on holiday (after having worked hard to save up the money to pay for it) and then end up with thousands of dollars in medical bills and debt.

If you will be out of the country for an extended period of time, be sure to check that your coverage covers you for the whole time away. Many travel insurance plans only cover you for three weeks and others up to nine weeks.

Group or Work Life Insurance

Many of the traditional and flex-benefit plans include life insurance coverage for the employee. Typically, the amount of life insurance coverage is equal to your annual income and can be increased to two or three times your annual income, with a cap on the total dollar amount payable.

This type of insurance is called "guaranteed yearly renewable term insurance," and when you leave the company, you no longer have coverage. In some instances you have an opportunity to purchase additional insurance benefit coverage and have it deducted from your paycheque. In situations like these I would strongly recommend that you look into what it would cost you to have your own personal life insurance coverage. There are a few reasons for this:

- If you leave the company, you will no longer have insurance coverage.
- When you purchase additional insurance coverage through your group plan, you tend to be significantly restricted in the amount and type of insurance you can purchase.
- The additional insurance you purchase may not be the most appropriate option.

One Frank Thought

When I prepare a financial plan for my clients, I recognize that they have group life insurance coverage, but I never take it into consideration because it is not guaranteed coverage. Should you leave your employer, or should you become sick and no longer able to work for your employer, you will no longer have the coverage, and you may no longer qualify for any coverage.

Guaranteed Insurability

Many group insurance policies permit employees, when they leave the company, to take their insurance coverage with them. In most instances they allow you to do this under the guise of what the insurance industry calls "guaranteed insurability." Guaranteed insurability means you are not asked any medical questions and do not have to go through any medical examinations. The insurance company simply guarantees that you have the coverage by signing a piece of paper.

In this situation, the insurance company takes a tremendous amount of risk. You could be terminally ill, and they will guarantee the coverage. Due to this increased risk, the premiums that they charge when you convert your life insurance from a company group policy to an individual policy under the guaranteed insurability clause are substantially higher than they would be if you were to go out and get insurance coverage on your own. So, provided you are relatively healthy, you are always better off to go out and purchase your own coverage.

One Frank Thought

When it comes to company group insurance coverage, I recommend that you take only the bare minimum, usually covered in the cost of the group benefits, and then go out and get your own policy that travels with you wherever you go and stays in force for as long as you continue to pay the premiums.

Group Pensions and Retirement Programs

If your company provides retirement or pension benefits, here is a little bit of information on defined benefit pension plans, defined contribution pension plans, group RRSPs, tax-free savings accounts (TFSAs), and employee stock purchase plans. (See Chapter 8 for more information.)

Defined Benefit Pension Plans (DBPPs)

Many would consider DBPPs to be traditional pension plans. These plans are almost always entirely funded by the employer, and the employee has no say in how the funds are invested. As the name states, they have a benefit that is defined. This is usually defined through a formulation of number of years of service and the age of the employee, multiplied by an average income and a percentage factor.

As the benefits or payout of the pension is defined, the liability of ensuring there is enough money in the pension to pay out all the pensioners falls on the company. It is because of this liability and the increasing costs of managing a pension plan that many companies are moving away from defined benefit plans toward defined contribution or group RRSP plans. Some companies are moving away from pension plans altogether.

Defined Contribution Pension Plans (DCPPs)

With these pension plans, the amount an employee contributes and the amount that the employer contributes is defined. In some of these plans, the employee has the choice of selecting among different investment styles or products. Typically, both the employer and the employee have an obligation to fund this on a regular basis, usually through payroll deductions. More often than not, DCPPs are not optional. With these plans, it is a little more difficult to project what your annual pension income might be. The total amount that is accumulated through employee and employer contributions, and the rate of return that is achieved on the investments, will determine how much money is available to fund your pension. It is important that you spend a bit of time reviewing your pension options to ensure that you are achieving the return necessary to fund the retirement lifestyle and goals that you'd like to achieve.

Group RRSPs

Group RRSPs are very similar to DCPPs. The amount that is contributed is known, but the amount that will be available to fund your retirement is not.

In many cases, these plans allow an employee to contribute up to the maximum RRSP contribution limit through the group plan into a series of investments, typically offered through banks or mutual fund companies. Many companies offer a matching program up to a certain amount. Typically, these can be 3% of income, up to a maximum of $2,500. Other matching programs may be a dollar-for-dollar matching program or $0.25 on the dollar (again, usually up to a maximum).

Group RRSPs offer the employee the greatest flexibility to do what they want with their retirement dollars. Also, they are far less expensive and easier to manage for the company. With reduced risk, liability costs, and administration for the company, it is no wonder that these types of plans are becoming a favourite. More and more companies find this to be the best alternative in providing retirement benefits for their employees. As an employee, it is up to you to take advantage of these programs. I strongly recommend that you participate in these plans *and get the free money!*

Let's look at an example. You work for a company that has a group RRSP program and the company will contribute $0.50 to your RRSP for every dollar that you contribute, up to a maximum of $2,500. You can elect to have $193 taken off every bi-weekly paycheque, and the company will contribute $96.

If you invested that money and earned an average of 7% over 30 years, you would accumulate $774,726 in RRSP savings. Of this amount, you would have contributed only $150,540 of your own earnings!

One Frank Thought

If you have an opportunity to participate in any of these plans, I strongly urge that you do so. Make an effort to structure your budget and have automatic deductions taken off your paycheque to ensure that you contribute the maximum amount to get the maximum free money available.

Tax-Free Savings Accounts (TFSAs)

Although still in their infancy, many companies are starting to offer their employees TFSAs as a way to save additional money. Some believe that companies looking to move away from pensions and retirement funding will offer only these new tax-free savings accounts.

In Chapter 8, you will learn more about retirement planning and how RRSPs and tax-free savings accounts can be used to fund your retirement. These new TFSAs can be very powerful tax-planning tools and resources. In order to benefit from these tax-planning benefits, you need to ensure that you start contributing on a regular basis early on.

If you have an option to contribute directly from payroll, and your budget allows it, you should choose to put money directly into your company's TFSA so you get used to not having the money while building the savings.

One Frank Thought

When you work through the exercises in Chapter 8 on retirement planning, a calculator will show you whether it makes more sense for you to contribute money to your RRSPs or to your tax-free savings accounts. This will enable you to make better decisions when participating.

Employee Stock Purchase Plans (ESPPs)

Some publicly traded companies allow employees to purchase company stock at a reduced rate or at a discount or average trading value. These plans can be very good and they can be very bad.

When considering investing in the company's stock, ask yourself these questions:

1. Do I believe the outlook for the company and the stock price is very good?
2. Does the investment in the stock match with my investment goals and objectives?
3. Do I have the funds to invest in the company stock?
4. Do I already have too much of my net worth invested in the company?

One Frank Thought

The last question is absolutely critical. I've seen many people who have their careers, pensions, savings, and investments all tied up in one company. This lack of diversification significantly increases their overall risk level.

I like to tell people the story of Enron, which once was considered to be one of the largest energy companies in the world. It employed thousands of people, was a blue-chip stock, and within eight short months went from trading at more than $100 a share to bankruptcy. Many Enron employees, including senior executives, were caught completely off guard. Not only did they lose their jobs, they lost their pensions, and many of them had participated in the employee stock purchase plan as well, because it was considered to be a company with good earnings and dividend payouts, and generally a conservative investment. These people lost everything! Their jobs, their retirement pensions, their investments, and savings—*everything!*

Be sure to spend some time reviewing your overall financial picture and calculate how much you have invested in various assets to ensure that you don't have too much of your money invested in one place.

Omar and Christine

When they got married, Christine and Omar set several goals for themselves, both as individuals and as a couple. These included starting to save for retirement and a down payment for a house, as well as taking care of themselves physically. They contacted me about organizing their finances, and I was thrilled to find out that they had already drafted a goals list. We worked on it to ensure that the goals were SMART, and then we developed a budget to help them reach their goals. While we were doing the budget, I asked them about the benefits their employers offered.

Christine is a chemical engineer who works for an oil-and-gas company in Calgary. Omar is in sales and works on commission. Their combined income is approximately $120,000. They met online two years ago and have been married for six months. They are both in their late twenties.

Christine has worked for her company since graduation; she loves the work and looks forward to being with the company for a long time. One of the things she loves about the company is the benefits program. Before she married Omar she had never really thought about her benefits, but now that there are two of them—and a possible family in the future—she appreciates how great it is to have benefits, unlike Omar's sales job, which has no benefits at his current level.

Omar won't have any benefits until he's earned significantly more money and is considered full-time. He does not anticipate this happening for another three years, when he will have built his contact list, and gained experience closing more deals.

Christine knew she had benefits but had never really investigated them, other than to make sure her dental bills were covered. I told her to read her benefits binder and talk to someone in the Human Resources department to ensure that she understood everything clearly. We made another appointment a month later to discuss her benefits and further define the plan they were creating.

At the next teleconference, Omar explained that the benefits research had helped them meet several of their goals, including a local gym membership. They discovered that one of Christine's benefits was a steep discount at a nearby workout chain. They had both been going to the gym at least twice a week in the morning before work and were enjoying this time together.

Not only were they working out, but Christine had also been seeing a nutritionist (thanks to her benefits coverage), who had determined that she had a gluten intolerance. Since then she had not eaten any wheat and was seeing real changes in her overall health.

Omar and Christine also had enjoyed a therapeutic massage after they learned that they each had coverage up to $500 per year. Massage, of course, is one of the most common benefits offered under extended health coverage and has proven stress-reduction benefits. They were feeling more relaxed than they had in years.

But this additional piece of news really caught my attention: her company offered a group RRSP program, and her employer would match up to $1,350 per year at her current salary. She visited her HR department and set up a biweekly deduction that was taken off of her paycheque automatically to maximize the matching program. The first deduction had come off the previous cheque and, with their careful budgeting, they weren't going to feel a pinch. They were now moving toward one of their major goals: a sizeable retirement fund.

I asked them about their other major goal: saving for a down payment on a house. They smiled and described what they had done. By reading the real estate section of the newspaper every weekend, they had identified the part of town they would like to live in. However, with Calgary experiencing record home prices, they didn't feel that it was the right time to buy in the area they wanted. Since they had no plans to start having children for a few more years, they were in no rush to buy. By staying on top of the market and waiting a few more years, they will have accumulated enough savings in their RRSP to take a first-time home buyers' loan and make a larger down payment.

I congratulated them on doing a great job of maximizing their benefits and moving toward each of their goals. I also mentioned that when they started planning to have children, they should look carefully at the benefits plan to determine the best way to arrange maternity/paternity leaves and income replacement. They promised to continue to get their free money.

Colleen and Tanya

Colleen and Tanya started dating in 1997 and moved in together two years later. In 2010 the couple moved from their native Ottawa to downtown Victoria, B.C., when Tanya was offered a substantial promotion within the software development company she had worked for since graduating from university. As a freelance editor, Colleen was able to retain many of her existing clients after the move and has already won several other good contracts on the West Coast.

Although they have decided not to marry formally, Colleen and Tanya have long been committed to spending the rest of their lives together. Colleen's family is extremely supportive of their relationship, but Tanya's parents have been significantly less accepting of Colleen's importance in their daughter's life.

Now that they've settled into their new surroundings, Colleen and Tanya have decided to make a fresh start with their finances. They'd already had two teleconferences with me, and we had refined and reshaped their goals list. At our next consultation we planned to look at the benefits Tanya was offered through her employer and make sure that the couple was using them to maximum effect. (Colleen, as a self-employed business owner, does not have benefits but is fully covered under Tanya's as her common-law partner.)

Tanya hadn't really reviewed her benefits since she first started working for the software company 16 years ago. I told her to source, from HR or from the company's intranet site, the most up-to-date benefits information available and to read carefully through it.

At the next teleconference, Tanya told me that she and Colleen had discovered, and had already started taking advantage of, some of the extended healthcare coverage included in her package. Colleen suffers from back pain caused by long hours at the computer and had been able to start having chiropractic treatment, covered by the benefits up to a certain dollar value. Tanya planned to take advantage of similar coverage to visit an acupuncturist, which she hopes will help with her recurring migraines.

I was pleased to see that Tanya had already taken full advantage of the group RRSP plan offered to her and was contributing $500 a month—the maximum amount that would be matched by her employer. One part of the RRSP benefit did concern me, however. Colleen was not named as the beneficiary, yet the couple had made it very clear in our previous meetings that each intended to leave all their assets to the other when they died. The same was true of Tanya's life insurance policy. When I asked about this, Tanya said that she had named Colleen as the beneficiary of both assets in her will. I advised them that anyone who wishes to pass their group benefit assets to a common-law partner should make certain that they name their partner as the beneficiary on the asset itself. This is to safeguard against a family member, usually one who does not agree with the relationship, from challenging the validity of the will and denying those benefits to the intended recipient. This seemed particularly important for Colleen and Tanya because Colleen did not have the support of Tanya's family. With Colleen as the named beneficiary on Tanya's policies, these assets would pass directly to Colleen outside of Tanya's estate—Tanya's family need not even be aware of them.

I also noticed that Tanya had life insurance coverage only through her employer. I explained that she would lose this immediately upon taking a job with a different company or if she should ever become sick and unable to work for the firm. I strongly recommended that they both arrange their own life insurance coverage, independent of the group coverage, that they would be able to keep regardless of their employment situation.

We identified one further saving during our call. Tanya's benefits included travel medical insurance, but in previous meetings, the couple had mentioned that they purchased an annual travel insurance package from a third party each year. We decided that it might be more cost-effective for them to stop purchasing the third party plan and to arrange non-medical coverage (e.g., for luggage, trip cancellation, etc.) for the individual trips that warranted it, if it wasn't covered by their credit card travel insurance.

By the end of this exercise, Tanya and Colleen were taking full advantage of the benefits available to them. They had protected Colleen against challenges to Tanya's will regarding her group RRSP and life insurance assets, and now they were aware of the limitations of group life insurance policies. They agreed to keep themselves up-to-date with all changes to the benefits package in future and to continue to take full advantage of the many ways the benefits could improve their lives.

Chapter Summary

- Be sure to thoroughly review your benefits, record the ones that are relevant to you, and keep them in an easy place for future reference.
- Understand how your benefits work with other benefits you receive, as well as those from other members of your family.
- Be sure that the benefits fit within your overall goals and objectives.
- Ensure that you're claiming all expenses and utilizing all benefits to their maximum.
- Make sure you understand any retirement benefits, pension plans, or other compensation arrangements . . . and get your free money!
- Sit down and review how these retirement and compensation arrangements fit within your overall investment and financial plans.

6

RISK AND LIVING INSURANCE

Risk appears when we are unprepared.

—Frank Wiginton

EVEN WITH THE BEST-LAID PLANS, unexpected things can happen. Trying to anticipate some of those problems can go a long way toward ensuring your success. As you work toward your goals, you may already be aware of some of the problems you might encounter in trying to achieve them. Inevitably, there will be one or more surprises or problems that you may not have planned for. Some of these problems you can manage and deal with, while others are out of your hands.

What I'm really talking about is *managing* risk. In order to accomplish our goals and deal with the mishaps along the way, we need to do our best to manage the risks involved.

Managing the Risk

Managing risk can be done in four different ways:

- Avoiding the risk
- Reducing the risk
- Sharing the risk
- Retaining some of the risk

Avoiding the Risk: This is as it says: changing what you are doing so that you no longer face the risk. An example might be to take public transit to work rather than driving. This avoids the risk of you being in a car accident.

Reducing the Risk: This involves taking actions to lessen the risk. If you do drive to work, you could reduce the risk of being in a car accident by slowing down or travelling outside of rush hour. It could even be something as drastic as moving closer to the office to shorten your drive.

One Frank Thought

Networking can be a great risk-reduction strategy by providing you with a wealth of resources to overcome any bump in the road. Whether you need to find a job, hire a competent contractor, or get a good deal on your next car purchase, networking can help you overcome the obstacle. If you are laid off, you run the risk of not having an income. Your network can reduce the risk of this happening. If you are not already on it, check out LinkedIn (www.linkedin.com) and start building your network!

Sharing the Risk: One example of sharing risk is purchasing car insurance and third-party liability coverage. By doing this, you share the financial risk with an insurance company. The insurance company shares its risk by providing coverage for many but only ever having to pay out for a few. A second example might be purchasing a company with another investor. If the company fails, you're in for only half or less of the loss.

Insurance is one of the easiest and cleanest ways to share risk. Whether it is a roadside assistance plan to help if your car breaks down, a furnace protection plan to replace your furnace in the dead of winter, or car/boat/home insurance to protect you from loss and litigation, insurance can offer you risk-sharing at an affordable price.

One Frank Thought

With the changes in home and auto insurance, I encourage everyone to make sure they have at least $1 million in liability protection, and for the few extra dollars it costs, you would be wise to get $2 million in liability protection.

Retaining Some of the Risk: This is when you are prepared to accept the consequences of an unforeseen event and deal with the repercussions. For example, if you are in a traffic accident, you may choose to pay for the damages yourself. You may decide to have a higher deductible on your insurance policy, in which case you've decided to retain the risk of incidental loss up to a certain amount. A broken window or a stolen laptop or bike may be misfortunes for which you retain the risk because the cost of fixing or replacing them would be less than the insurance deductible.

Only you can decide if you can avoid risk by not doing something, but many would agree you could greatly reduce the risk simply through education, planning, preparation, and practice. When you do decide to do something, figure out how much of the known risk you are willing to retain and determine if there are ways to share it.

Living Insurance: Insurance that Pays Out to Help You Live!

Managing risks that are beyond our control falls under the category of sharing the risk. Some of the most impactful events on our financial lives and the lives of our families are death, critical illness, disability, and the loss of independence. These catastrophic events can create substantial hardship for us and our loved ones and frequently happen without warning.

To mitigate the risks that we cannot predict or control, we look to the various insurance products and solutions that exist: life insurance in the event we die; critical illness insurance in case we suffer from a serious illness, such as a heart attack, stroke, or cancer; disability insurance against the chance of a debilitating incident that prevents us from working; and long-term care insurance in the event we are no longer able to take care of ourselves.

I have met many people over the years who are substantially under-insured and consequently open to significant financial risk and hardship. I have met others who have too much insurance or have established insurance that does not apply to their situation or who simply have the wrong kind of insurance to meet their goals.

First off, for those of you reading this book and who have a negative impression of insurance, I need you to keep an open mind and remember that I am not here to sell you anything. I am presenting this information purely to inform you, the reader, about insurance and its uses.

Second, I want all readers to stop thinking of insurance as a financial burden and start thinking of it as a financial tool. Once you start thinking about it in the context of another investment product, you will understand how you (not the insurance company) can benefit and prosper from using this investment vehicle.

Let's take a look at some of the different types of insurance and the pros and cons of each. As well, let's look at some of the different options available to enhance and improve the insurance to help you meet your goals.

Critical Illness Insurance

Although death is inevitable, you are five times more likely to suffer from a critical illness before the age of 65 than you are to die before that age. The three most common forms of critical illness include heart attack, stroke, and cancer. Most critical illness insurance policies provide coverage for anywhere from 10 to 30 different critical illnesses.

Here's how it works: should you be diagnosed with an illness covered by your policy and survive (typically) 30 days, the insurance company will pay you a tax-free lump sum. (If you do not survive the 30 days, many policies will repay the premiums you have paid.) Upon the tax-free payout of the policy, you are free to take this money and do whatever you want with it.

For example, let's say you purchased a $100,000 critical illness policy. You went to the doctor last week, and the doctor found a lump in your throat and referred you to a specialist to have it tested. Today you received the frightening call that it is indeed cancer. Thirty days from now, the insurance company will write a cheque to you in the amount of $100,000, provided you are still alive. You can do whatever you wish with these funds. You could use them to pay for the best medical treatment in the world, you could start taking all the trips that you've always wanted to take, or you could decide to throw the biggest party anyone's ever seen. It's entirely up to you.

There is a statistical probability that some of us will suffer a stroke and become disabled. On the payout of critical illness insurance, you could use the money to retrofit your house or purchase a new house that is more suitable for a wheelchair. Or you may choose to use some of the funds to pay for a full-time nurse to take care of you, or you may simply decide to pay off existing debts.

Critical illness insurance policies allow you to purchase additional riders (add-ons). Riders include paid-up-by-a-certain-age, according to which, once you reach, say, 55 you no longer have to pay for the insurance, and the policy stays in force. Another is a return-of-premium (ROP) rider, according to which, after a certain time has elapsed, you can choose to cancel the policy and get all of the premiums you paid returned to you. This creates a sort of forced saving in the best-case scenario.

Here is a sample list of the types of illness that can be covered by a policy. Be sure to check the type of coverage a policy has. Often a cheaper policy won't cover you for as many illnesses.

1. Cancer
2. Heart attack
3. Stroke
4. Coronary artery bypass surgery
5. Kidney failure
6. Major organ transplant or failure
7. Aortic surgery
8. Heart valve replacement
9. Benign brain tumour
10. Blindness

11. Deafness

12. Paralysis

13. Multiple sclerosis

14. Severe burns

15. Coma

16. Loss of speech

17. Loss of limbs

18. Motor neuron disease

19. Alzheimer's disease

20. Parkinson's disease

21. Occupational HIV

22. Coronary angioplasty

23. Stage A (T1a or T1b) prostate cancer

24. Stage 1A malignant melanoma

25. Ductal carcinoma in situ of the breast

26. Extended disability

27. Loss of independent existence

Critical illness policies that provide for a loss of independence (when you are unable to perform two of six specified daily functions: feeding yourself, bathing yourself, dressing yourself, using the bathroom, bladder and bowel continence, and transferring yourself from bed or chair) can be used to cover the costs of long-term care. In some instances, should you keep a critical illness policy in force long-term, it may end up becoming a long-term care insurance policy by default through the loss of independence coverage.

Disability Insurance Coverage

Disability insurance is designed to replace your income from employment or self-employment in the event that you are no longer able to work. It pays out a monthly benefit, tax-free, and is typically a percentage of what you earned before becoming disabled. The benefits may last for a few years— and possibly until you're ready to retire, if you can't go back to your old job or to any job.

Many company benefit plans offer short- and long-term disability insurance. They typically offer somewhere between 50 and 65% of income in the event that you become disabled. You must qualify on a continual basis for your long-term disability coverage. This means that you must prove your disability on an ongoing basis to continue to qualify for your monthly benefits.

Your Own Occupation vs. Any Occupation

Companies offering disability insurance look at and consider whether or not you can do any job or the same job you were doing prior to the disabling event. If you purchase disability insurance with the condition of being able to continue the same occupation, it typically is more expensive than insurance covering you in case you cannot continue with any occupation. With the "any occupation" provision, if you are deemed capable of earning a living doing any job, then you will no longer qualify for benefits. An example might be the case of a surgeon who developed Parkinson's disease and so was unable to control the movement of her hands: she would be considered disabled and unable to perform her own occupation, but, as many with Parkinson's have proven, she could still find gainful employment and function within society.

How Much Coverage Should You Have?

To determine the amount of disability insurance coverage that would be appropriate, you need to consider several factors. As disability insurance is paid out on a tax-free basis (when the premiums are paid with after-tax dollars), you should seriously consider your net income rather than your gross income when determining the amount of coverage you will require. Other things to consider include the quality of life you wish to have and the additional costs associated with the disability, such as renovating a house for wheelchair access, moving into a more accessible home, purchasing a customized vehicle, increased medical costs, employing private nurses, and hiring people to clean and maintain your property.

On the flip side, you will likely have a lower tax rate and additional tax deductions, such as medical and disability tax credits. As well, other lifestyle expenses are likely to decrease.

Employment Insurance Sickness Benefit and Canada Pension Plan Disability Benefit

The Employment Insurance Sickness Benefit is payable to those who are off work for medical reasons for a short period of time. You can receive 55% of your income up to a maximum of $485 a week for up to 15 weeks. This small amount is meant to provide you with short-term disability coverage in the event that you do not have group benefits or any other benefits.

The Canada Pension Plan Disability Benefit is meant for long-term disabilities and starts when the EI benefits end. To qualify, your disability must be severe and prolonged, and you must not be able to perform *any* occupation. The average payout is approximately $850 a month and the maximum an individual could qualify for in 2012 was $1,185 a month. You must have contributed to CPP in four of the last six years. Your CPP disability benefit will continue as long as you are unable to earn money in any occupation or until you reach age 65, when you will begin to receive your regular CPP retirement benefit.

An Example

Sam earns $45,000 a year, gross. After income taxes and CPP and EI deductions, Sam's net income is about $32,000. Sam will likely qualify for approximately $900 a month in CPP disability benefits, which after tax nets out at $8,800 a year. This leaves him short $23,200, which is approximately 50% of his gross income. Should he decide that he would need additional income to cover increased expenses due to a disability, Sam may wish to add an additional $8,000 a year in coverage, leaving him a net shortfall of $31,200. He will need approximately 70% of his gross income in after-tax dollars from a disability insurance policy.

One Frank Thought

You are more likely to suffer a critical illness than you are a disability. Many critical illnesses can cause disabilities, so you may decide to go with a smaller amount of disability coverage (50% of income) and offset the loss of income with the lump sum, tax-free payout that you would get from your critical illness insurance policy.

Long-Term Care Insurance

When most people think of long-term care insurance, they think of getting old and having to go into an old-age home. This really isn't surprising because the majority of people who require long-term care are over the age of 70. However, there are many situations where younger people require long-term care, and they typically need it for much longer than seniors. Imagine a 25-year-old woman getting into a car accident that leaves her requiring long-term care. This is care she may need for 60 years or more, whereas someone who is 60, 65, or 70 may require care for only a few months or years.

Long-term care insurance is meant to provide a monthly or annual payment to cover the additional costs of long-term care through a recognized institution or nurse practitioner. Not surprisingly, this can cost a significant amount of money, adding up to thousands of dollars a month. These costs and expenses are only likely to increase for the following reasons:

- Rising medical costs
- Reductions in healthcare subsidies by the government
- Increased demand for long-term care as the large baby-boom demographic gets older, thereby reducing the number of spaces available

The laws of economics tell us that when there is a significant increase in demand and a limited supply, the cost will rise significantly.

When considering getting long-term care insurance, you need to do some research into the costs involved and look at your own financial situation to see what assets you have that could be used to help cover those costs. One other thing to consider is the rising cost of inflation.

One Frank Thought

My personal opinion is that we will likely see an annual increase in the cost of long-term care of between 5 and 10% over the next 35 years. This means that a long-term care costs that are currently $5,000 a month could be as much as $20,000 a month 20 years from now. This may seem extreme, but it is not unrealistic.

As you go through this process of getting your personal finances in order, it is essential that you look at and consider protecting yourself from financial hardship. Life insurance, as we will discuss in the next chapter, is one thing, but when you die, your personal expenses die with you. If you suffer a critical illness or disability, your personal expenses still exist, and will likely increase while your income decreases. This double threat is why *living insurance* can be such an important part of your personal financial success.

If you don't want to avoid a risk—by never driving a car, for example— be sure to reduce the risk by slowing down and travelling safely. As well, share the risk by ensuring you have proper insurance to cover those unforeseeable events.

Kyle

Kyle has worked at the same mid-sized mining company since he graduated from university a decade ago. As a mining inspector, he travels to his company's sites all over Canada. Although he makes the occasional trip to Ontario or the head office in British Columbia, he still lives in Flin Flon, just down the street from his parents, and conducts most of his land and property inspections in Manitoba.

About a year ago, he was inspecting a mine near Flin Flon when a pile of scrap metal shifted and he cut his leg on an old pipe. The proper procedure was to fill out an accident report, and, even though he thought it was a fuss over nothing, he finished the inspection and went to see the company nurse to get the proper form. The nurse handed him a huge document to fill out for his tiny cut; they both laughed, and he filled out the report before heading home.

Before he went to bed that night, he looked at the cut and noticed a bit of pus and blood seeping out. He wasn't too worried about it but put some hydrogen peroxide and a bit of antiseptic ointment on it, just in case. Unfortunately, the infection grew worse, and the next day he was at the doctor's office getting an antibiotic to deal with the infection. One week and two different types of antibiotic later, it was worse. He also began to experience nausea and tingling in his hands and feet. He told no one. Almost a week after the original injury, he stood up from his desk and passed out. When he regained consciousness, one of his co-workers was calling an ambulance.

After blood work and a thorough examination of his leg—now bright red from mid-thigh down to his foot—the doctor told him bluntly that his body was in septic shock due to a staph infection. Even worse, the infection had attacked his kidneys. Unfortunately, the local hospital did not have the resources to treat him, and he needed to be airlifted to Winnipeg immediately.

He doesn't remember everything that happened because he was on painkillers and massive doses of antibiotics. His parents had to fly to Winnipeg and keep him informed throughout the whole ordeal. The infection in his leg had progressed so far that, by the time he arrived in Winnipeg, the doctors had no choice but to amputate. Kyle also experienced kidney failure as part of the septic shock.

A year later Kyle has mostly recovered. He is back at home in Flin Flon and out of the wheelchair that was his constant companion for several months. In fact, he had the temporary ramps in his house removed just last week, and his last dialysis treatment was two months ago. He has almost completely adjusted to the artificial leg, thanks to a lot of physiotherapy, and he expects to return to his job as an inspector in about a month—as long as there are no setbacks.

There are a few key things that Kyle did that helped him to get through this ordeal. He took the time to fill out the accident report. As a result, the Workers' Compensation Board (WCB) covered his period of disability and his job has been guaranteed. The support he received through WCB was topped up by the disability insurance that kicked in when he needed 24-hour nursing care and spent two months at a long-term care facility. The disability insurance replaced about 50% of his gross income and was tax-free.

Kyle had also purchased an optional critical illness policy through his work when he was 31 and, fortunately, it covered kidney failure. A month after the amputation, while he was in rehab learning to walk with his new leg, he received a tax-free, lump sum payment of $75,000. Although he joked with me that his first impulse was to take a trip, he used a large portion of the money to pay for nursing care, physiotherapy, ramps for his house, and his mortgage payments while he was on leave. Thanks to his disability insurance, workers' compensation, and critical illness insurance, he was able to focus on his recovery instead of worrying about his future and his home.

He mentioned that when he bought the critical illness insurance, he couldn't imagine ever needing it, but now he considers it the best investment he has ever made. He concluded, "Life is too risky not to have protection." I couldn't agree more.

David and Sheila

David and Sheila have done everything right to ensure they have peace of mind. Now in their forties, they have steady, secure jobs with full benefits at a local manufacturing company. They have contributed and invested fully into their pensions and set up wills and powers of attorney to ensure that the surviving spouse and their three children will be taken care of when either David or Sheila are gone.

At least, they thought they had taken care of everything.

I received a call from Sheila a few years ago, and I could tell that something wasn't right: her normally cheerful tone was absent. I asked her what was wrong and she started crying. After some reassuring words, she told me that six months earlier, her 70-year-old mother, Beth, had suffered a stroke and lost the use of most of the right side of her body. She was out of the hospital but could no longer take care of herself. Sheila moved her mother in with the family and, with the help of her kids and David, had become a full-time caregiver. It was taking everything she had just to get through each day, and she didn't know how she was going to make it through another couple of months.

What was really troubling her was that Beth did not have anything other than her small pension, CPP, and Old Age Security to pay for her medical needs. The long-term care facilities in Truro were so much in demand that there was a long waiting list for all of them. Sheila didn't see any way out of the situation other than to pay for nursing care until a space opened up. Sheila was currently on caregiver's leave and receiving EI, but that would soon run out and she would have to go back to work.

She told me that she didn't ever want her kids to have to deal with this type of situation, and she was hoping I could help. She had heard something about long-term care insurance and was wondering if that would solve the problem. Two days later, we had a teleconference to talk about their insurance options. I started by explaining the pros and cons of long-term care insurance. It covers monthly or annual expenses arising from long-term care, either when the patient is living at home or is in an institution. However, for most policies, you have to submit receipts, and the types of care that are covered can be limited.

Then we examined Sheila and David's situation. They had fully invested in the pension plan through their workplace, and after they retired they would be receiving a nice income that would help pay for long-term care, even with the likely increases in inflation. Additionally, they would be mortgage-free by the time they retired, and the sale of their home, or a secured line of credit, would likely pay for any financial shortfalls related to long-term care. However, Sheila disagreed with this arrangement completely: she didn't want to have to sell their home to pay for care. I agreed and explained that they could own a policy that would allow both of them to move into a retirement residence so they could be together, rather than require one to stay in their home alone.

Finally, they both had critical illness policies that we had arranged five years earlier. These 30-year policies would cover them up until retirement, at which point their premiums would be returned if there had been no claims. This policy had a feature called loss of independence that guaranteed a lump sum payout if they lost the ability to perform the activities associated with daily living.

Sheila gasped and admitted she had forgotten about that rider. The mood of our call changed as she realized they were well covered.

I finished with this advice: insurance is meant to give us peace of mind, and if, after all I had told them, they were still anxious and wanted long-term care insurance, then we would figure out a way to make it work with their budget. I also suggested that they not make any decisions while Sheila was under such tremendous stress. Eventually, Sheila and David did decide to purchase Term-100, long-term care insurance. Since they were both healthy and fairly young, we were able to get reasonable premiums through a trusted insurance broker whom I work with regularly.

Chapter Summary

- Take some time to prepare and plan before doing different activities.
- Identify the potential obstacles and risks and decide how to deal with them (avoid, reduce, share, or retain).
- Review and understand your current insurance policies to ensure you have sufficient and proper coverage.
- Speak with your benefit provider to understand what type of insurance protection you have and how it works. (If your work disability insurance coverage is for any occupation, you may wish to purchase supplementary coverage to have own occupation coverage.)
- Through an independent insurance broker, evaluate the different types of living insurance that make sense for your personal situation.

7

LIFE INSURANCE

When paying for insurance, the premiums always seem too much and the payout never seems enough.

—Anonymous

LIFE INSURANCE CAN BE A difficult subject. Thinking about what happens when you or someone you love dies can provoke strong emotions. But thinking about what would happen to the people you love if you were to die should help you to understand why life insurance is such an important part of a proper and responsible financial plan. Insurance is a tool that provides you with peace of mind, the knowledge that you will never leave behind worry, anxiety, or financial stress. It is never meant to replace a loved one, but instead to protect the loved ones left behind.

The reality is that many people are under-insured and should something happen to them, they are putting their loved ones at risk of financial distress, and possibly poverty. I like to believe that it is only a lack of knowledge and understanding that is causing those individuals to put their loved ones in that situation. As you go through this chapter, you will learn about the different types of life insurance and the options that exist to fit your needs. I also take you through some alternative ways to use insurance to reduce your investment risk and taxes.

How Much Life Insurance Do You Need?

There are two methods for calculating the amount of life insurance needed to provide for those you leave behind: the income-replacement method and the expense-elimination method.

Income Replacement

This method is designed to replace the income that was lost when the insured person died. In order to properly and efficiently determine how much income is needed, you first need to understand how much income is being generated by the individual being insured.

Let's look at a simple example: Catherine and her husband, John, both work; they have two children, aged 3 and 5. Catherine earns $100,000 a year before taxes. After tax, Catherine's income is about $72,000 a year. From this amount, the family determines that the expenses that are solely Catherine's total about $16,000 a year, leaving the family $56,000. This means that if something should happen to Catherine, the loss of income to the family would be about $56,000 a year.

Under the income-replacement method, it would be necessary to have sufficient insurance to generate an after-tax income of $56,000 a year for the family. Assuming the life insurance proceeds are invested and generate an after-tax rate of return of 4.5%, Catherine would need approximately $1 million in life insurance coverage to replace the loss of her $56,000-a-year income for the next 35 years.

One Frank Thought

People often neglect to take inflation into consideration when determining the amount of life insurance they need. In 30 years, $56,000 will be worth only $24,000 in buying power given a 3% inflation rate. To make up for this loss, Catherine would need to increase her life insurance coverage to a little more than $1.5 million.

Expense Elimination

This method would see that all the family's expenses are paid off or paid up upon the insured person's death. This would include any and all debt, such as credit cards and lines of credit or mortgages. This may also include money to pay for children's activities, such as music lessons, sports camp, and tutoring. Other major expenses would include children's education, new vehicles, vacation properties, and family vacations. Once lifestyle expenses are paid for, additional funds will likely be needed to cover day-to-day expenses, such as food, utilities, property taxes, and insurance premiums. Other expenses that are typically missed or ignored include increased taxation in retirement for the surviving spouse due to a loss of income-splitting. Using this method, there is much less of a need for an annual income to be generated from the proceeds of the insurance policy. This is primarily due to the fact that the expenses of the family are dramatically reduced or eliminated. Other benefits include lower taxation on investment returns from the insurance proceeds, as well as less erosion due to inflation.

Both of these methods are perfectly viable, and it should be your preference that determines which method you use. Be sure to use the life insurance needs analysis tool on the website to determine whether you have sufficient life insurance protection or not.

Self-Employed?

Although issues related to self-employment are beyond the scope of this book, here is a little bit of information. Be sure to work with your financial planner to better understand how insurance can benefit you as a business owner.

Self-employed individuals need to protect their stake in their businesses. Here's how life insurance can be used:

1. As collateral for a business loan, sometimes at the request of the financial institution making the loan. If it is necessary to assign the policy as security, a portion of the premium will be deductible as a business expense.
2. To fund a buy–sell agreement to provide surviving partners or shareholders with the cash to buy out the deceased's share and to keep the business going.
3. To insure the key people in the company. Life insurance is often used as a safeguard against financial loss to the business caused by death of the owner, a partner, or a key employee.

4. To provide protection to the business owner's family against the debts of the company. Unless the company is set up as a limited company, the individual (and his/her estate) assumes full personal responsibility for the business debts.

Life Insurance

There are two forms of life insurance: permanent and term. Permanent life insurance is, as it says, permanent. Once the policy is in force and you pay your premiums, the policy is guaranteed to pay out. Term insurance has the same guarantee of payout but only for the specified term of the policy.

Permanent Insurance

The two most common forms of permanent insurance coverage are whole life and universal life. The premiums on these policies are usually level (i.e., they don't go up), and the payout is guaranteed.

Whole Life Insurance

Whole Life Insurance provides both life coverage and a savings component. The savings portion is called "cash value" and builds over time with each premium payment. If you choose to cancel your policy, then you are entitled to this built-up cash value. You may also borrow against the cash value in the form of a policy loan, giving you access to the money without having to give up your life insurance coverage. Upon death, both the cash value (minus any outstanding loans against it) and the policy amount pay out to your beneficiaries tax-free.

Pros:
- Policy never expires.
- Guaranteed to pay out.
- Cash value grows tax-free.
- Cash value is protected from creditors.
- Cash value can be used as collateral.

Cons:
- Higher premiums.
- Investment return on cash value within the policy is based on a fixed interest rate (typically lower than if you invested it yourself).

- You must cancel the policy to take your cash value out (if you decide not to borrow against the cash value).

Who should use whole life insurance? I really don't know. There may be someone for whom this form of insurance is appropriate, but I can't figure out who.

One Frank Thought

I have spent many hours speaking with agents and brokers who sell insurance, and none of them can give me a good reason why anyone would purchase whole life insurance. When you have the ability to purchase guaranteed insurance coverage through other types of policies with greater flexibility and features, there does not seem to be a need to ever purchase a whole life policy. (One thing I did learn was that the agents get paid a much bigger commission for selling whole life than other types of policies.)

Universal Life Insurance

Universal Life Insurance combines life insurance coverage with the option to invest in a portfolio of investments. This flexibility makes this type of insurance a more attractive option than whole life insurance. If you choose to cancel your policy, then you are entitled to the built-up investment savings. You may also cash out the investment assets (without cancelling the policy) or use them to pay the policy fees going forward until the funds run out. Upon death, both the accumulated investment assets and the policy amount pay out to your beneficiaries tax-free.

Pros:
- Policy never expires.
- Guaranteed to pay out.
- Premiums never increase.
- Broader selection of investment options.
- Investments grow tax-deferred.
- Investments are protected from creditors.
- The policy holder can withdraw investments without cancelling the policy.

Con:
- Higher premiums in the short term.

Temporary Insurance

The two most common forms of temporary insurance coverage are term and group benefit insurance. The premiums are much less expensive than permanent policies and tend to expire before paying out.

Term Life

This type of life insurance policy expires after a period of time (typically 10 or 20 years). These policies do not carry an investment component, and the premiums tend to be much lower than either whole life or universal life insurance policies in the short term.

Pros:
- Substantially lower premiums.
- Opportunity to align insurance coverage with life events (e.g., if you have a 20-year mortgage, or if you have young children, you could purchase a 20-year term insurance policy).

Cons:
- Expires worthless at the end of the term.
- No investment or tax sheltering.
- Premiums increase substantially on renewal.

One Frank Thought

Many people, including many agents who sell life insurance, believe that term insurance is the best option. They say, "Okay, I need to get insurance. What's the cheapest thing out there?" What they're missing is the fact that life insurance can be used for many purposes beyond the immediate purpose. If it is determined that you need to have life insurance for longer than the term, you may be wise to take advantage of the benefits of universal life insurance.

Term 100

This type of policy is kind of a hybrid between permanent and term insurance. Simply put, this is a term insurance policy to age 100. As the majority of us will not likely see age 100 it, in a sense, becomes a permanent insurance policy. Should you live to be 100, the insurance policy will usually be paid up. So you no longer have to pay for the policy, and the policy will pay out on your death.

Pros:
- Typically, the cost is a little less than the cost of permanent insurance.
- It gives you the comfort of knowing that you will have insurance protection for as long as you want it.
- It does not expire the way a term policy does.

Cons:
- It provides life insurance coverage only, with no opportunity to invest within the policy the way you can with a permanent insurance policy.
- There's no way to shelter assets from taxes and creditors as there is with a permanent policy.
- It cannot be paid up.

Insurable Interest

To purchase life insurance, you must have an *insurable interest*. This means that you must have a connection with or a valid reason for insuring the person. So, in most cases, this person will be a family member or business partner. The insurance companies do not allow you to purchase life insurance on strangers or people at arm's length to you as this would increase the chance of them having an untimely death. The ability of a person to buy insurance on the life of a stranger would create a *moral hazard* wherein the person owning the insurance policy stands to profit from the death of the insured.

Different Ways to Set Up a Life Insurance Policy

There are essentially four different ways an insurance policy can be set up. The policy can be written for a group, on an individual, on a couple based on the first death, or on a couple based on the last death. Let's take a look at the pros and cons of each.

Group Life Insurance

Group Life Insurance is a very common type of policy that covers people who belong to group benefit plans through their work or association. Some of these group plans allow people the opportunity to purchase additional coverage. This typically comes in the form of X dollars per $10,000 worth of coverage. Although it seems as if it's a very inexpensive option, it is actually one of the most expensive forms of life insurance. Many group life insurance policies provide what is known as yearly renewable term coverage. Essentially, this means that you are purchasing life insurance based on your age for one year; at the end of that year, the insurance company increases the premiums due to the fact that you are one year older. What makes this type seem inexpensive is that the insurance company provides it at a discount based on it being part of group coverage, plus there are many contributors, including the company itself, to cover the cost of the few who will pass away during their employment. What most people don't consider is that all the coverage they have while they are working for the company disappears when they leave the company.

Pros:
- Coverage with no medical or health questionnaire.
- Relatively inexpensive and very easy to set up.

Cons:
- Limited amount of coverage (typically two times your annual income to a maximum of $250,000).
- Costs go up every year.
- No longer have coverage when you leave the company or are fired from the company.
- May not be able to qualify for life insurance when you leave the company and, therefore, may end up with no coverage at all.
- If given the option to take life insurance with you when you leave, it will be at the highest rate.

Individual Policy

This is the most common type of life insurance policy. Typically, an individual will apply for life insurance and have a policy written on their life or the life of another individual, such as a spouse, child, or business partner.

Pros:
- The policy remains on the individual regardless of any change in relationship status.
- The ownership of the policy is transferable.
- The insured individual is the only one who needs to go through health screening.

Con:
- The cost of insurance may be slightly higher than for a joint first- or joint last-to-die policy.

Joint First-to-Die

This type of insurance policy is typically purchased by spouses and pays out when the first one dies. Both individuals being insured must go through medical screening.

Pros:
- May mean that the couple has to have only one insurance policy to provide the necessary protection for the family.
- Cost of insurance may be lower than purchasing two individual insurance policies.
- May allow a couple to purchase a greater amount of life insurance to protect the family.

Cons:
- Insurance cannot be taken with you upon the dissolution of the relationship.
- Cannot be used for estate-planning purposes upon second death as it will have already paid out.

Joint Last-to-Die

This type of insurance policy is typically purchased by spouses and pays out when the last one dies. Both individuals being insured must go through medical screening.

> Pros:
> - Very effective tool for estate planning.
> - Typically less expensive than individual policies.
> - Can be used to create a larger estate than individual policies alone.
>
> Cons:
> - Cost of the insurance may become a burden to the surviving spouse.
> - Cannot be converted to an individual policy on dissolution of the relationship.

For a Child

Life insurance on a child is an individual insurance policy. In many cases there is little need to insure a child as the child does not generate income for the family.

> Pros:
> - Cost of insurance for a child is typically very low.
> - Helps to ensure insurability, i.e., the child can qualify for insurance before any medical issues arise.
> - May provide additional tax-sheltering and estate-planning opportunities for the parents.
>
> Cons:
> - Additional financial burden for the family that may not be needed.
> - Should the child pass away, the payout adds little value or comfort to the family.

Key Person

This type of insurance is typically aimed at business owners and senior executives of companies. Its purpose is to help support the business should a key person pass away. The funds may be used to help find a suitable replacement and/or buy back the share ownership from the insured's estate or family.

Pros:
- Protects the business from financial loss or ruin during a critical time.
- Can ensure that the management and running of the company does not fall into the hands of an individual who does not have the skills or knowledge necessary to make it a success.

Con:
- Cost of insurance for small businesses or business start-ups may eat into cash flow and jeopardize the success of the company.

One Frank Thought

I really don't like *mortgage life insurance* that is offered through your mortgage provider. Although very simple to apply for, you aren't underwritten until a claim is made. This is to say that there is no guarantee of payout. The other issue is that although your premiums never rise, the amount of coverage (your mortgage balance) continuously declines. I would much rather see you get your own permanent or even term insurance policy than purchase mortgage insurance.

Insurance Riders or Add-Ons

Whichever type of policy you choose, there are additional features you can add to the policy to make it fit better with your goals and objectives. These are called "riders." Here are some of the most common ones:

Paid Up or Limited Pay

These two options are typically applied to permanent life insurance policies to restrict the number of years in which you have to pay for the policy. Essentially, you pay a higher premium up front and then, after a certain point in time, you no longer have to pay any insurance premiums. So the policy is paid up, or you only have a limited time to pay premiums.

Pros:
- The total cost of insurance is known.
- Allows you to plan your expenses better for the long term.
- Allows you to determine more precisely the rate of return on the policy.

Cons:
- Cost of the policy is higher in the short term.
- Should the insured pass away prematurely, you may have paid more than you had to.

Return of Premium

You can add this option to a policy to allow you to get back all the money you've paid in premiums on the payout of the policy or should you decide to cancel it. This is used on some life insurance policies but is more commonly used on critical illness insurance products.

Pros:
- Very little risk to taking out the insurance as you will receive all your premiums back at the end of the term or when you decide to cancel the policy.
- Allows you to have insurance coverage and, if you never make a claim, it essentially becomes a forced savings account.

Cons:
- No interest or rate of return is paid on these funds.
- It increases the cost of insurance.
- If the policy pays out it does not pay out, the additional premiums paid for the return–of-premium option.*

---

* With some insurance products, the return of premium gets added to the face value of the policy year after year, and upon payout of the face amount, the return of premium that has accumulated in the account also pays out.

Guaranteed Convertibility

This option is for term insurance products and provides the owner the opportunity to convert the policy to a permanent policy at any point without the insured having to go through additional medical screening. The caveat to this is that the price for the permanent policy is based on the insured's age at the time of conversion.

Pros:
- Ensures that an individual can get permanent insurance coverage even in the event of a medical condition, without the fear of the term insurance expiring.
- Allows someone who is applying for insurance, but is unsure whether or not to go with permanent insurance, the opportunity to change their mind at a later date.

Cons:
- Option to convert typically expires at a certain age.
- May add a small additional premium to the cost of the policy.
- The cost of the new guaranteed insurance coverage is at the insured person's attained age and, therefore, will be more expensive than purchasing permanent insurance at the outset.

Guaranteed Renewability

This option is typically for term insurance products and provides the owner the opportunity to renew the term coverage without the insured person having to go through additional medical screening. This option is becoming pretty standard among the various term life insurance products.

Pros:
- Guarantees that even if you suffer from a medical condition during the initial term, you can continue with term coverage at the end of that initial term.
- Can provide additional peace of mind in knowing that you can continue to have insurance coverage over a longer period of time.

Con:

• The cost of insurance upon renewal will typically be higher than if you went through a new medical underwriting (provided your health has not changed).

Buy Term Insurance and Invest the Difference?

This is a very common expression you will hear among those who predominantly sell term insurance policies. They will explain to you that the cost of permanent insurance is too high, and that you could take the difference between the cost of permanent insurance and the cheaper cost of term insurance, invest it, and make some financial gains. The problem with this theory is that it doesn't take into account what you plan to use the insurance for. If you are using the insurance for a very short period of time—let's say 10 years—then, yes, you may be better off buying term insurance and investing the difference.

When they look at their insurance needs in the context of a comprehensive financial plan, many people find that they have a need for their life insurance well beyond a period of 10 or even 20 years. In some cases, as you'll read below, life insurance can be used quite effectively for estate-planning purposes. If this is the case, then permanent insurance is not only substantially cheaper in the long run but also a much better investment.

To illustrate this, I have taken an actual quote from the least expensive insurance provider at the time of writing for a 35-year-old, non-smoking male and made a 50-year comparison of the cost of a $100,000 life insurance policy. The chart below shows how, with 20-year term insurance, the cost of insurance increases dramatically in years 21 and 41, whereas the cost of the permanent insurance stays level throughout the life of the insured.

Over the course of 50 years, the term insurance coverage costs approximately $101,700 for $100,000 of coverage, whereas the cost of the permanent insurance (although more expensive initially) is only a total of $25,000 over 50 years.

If the insured were to buy term insurance, invest the difference, and get an 8% annual return year in and year out, at the end of 45 years, they would be no better off than if they had purchased the permanent insurance. At the end of 50 years, they would be more than $30,000 behind. Note: this does not take into consideration the tax burden that would be created by the investment account (which would only make the term insurance a worse option).

One Frank Thought

What I've heard many times throughout my career is that fewer than 2% of all term insurance policies ever pay out. The main reason for this is that people outlive the original term and/or cancel the policy because they no longer need it or because the premiums become too expensive.

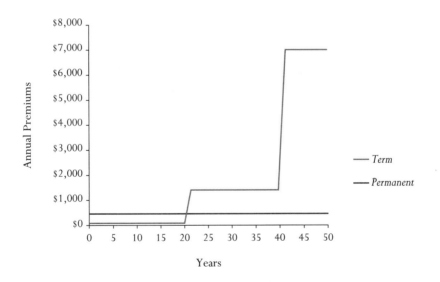

Year	Annual Premiums		Investments
	Permanent	Term	
1 - 20	$500	$160	$16,789
21 - 40	$500	$1,425	$32,537
41 - 50	$500	$7,000	$-34,450
Total	**$25,000**	**$101,700**	

One Frank Thought

I am a big proponent of permanent insurance. It's what my wife and I have. The way we look at it is that our family will definitely get back more than we pay in. We recognize that there is a higher cost initially for the insurance, but we have put it into our budget and found ways to manage. Everyone's situation is different, and I would rather you have *sufficient coverage* by using term insurance than by going with the more expensive permanent insurance and not having enough coverage.

Affordability

Now, some of you may be saying that you agree that permanent insurance is a better option, but the additional cost would stretch your budget too far. In these instances, I usually recommend that people take out a blended coverage—some permanent and some term. Maybe you determine that you need about $500,000 worth of life insurance. You may decide to take out $200,000 worth of permanent coverage and $300,000 worth of term coverage. This combination, or any combination thereof, can be arranged to meet your budget and also your coverage needs.

Additional Uses for Life Insurance

Life insurance can be used for many purposes beyond protecting income in the event someone dies. Here are a few other ways life insurance can be used.

Creating a Legacy: For some people, leaving a sum of money to their loved ones or to their favourite charities or organizations is important. When living on a fixed income through retirement, a concern is whether or not you will outlive your money. By purchasing permanent insurance, you can budget and set aside the premiums necessary to pay for a policy that is guaranteed to pay out upon your death. This ensures you can achieve your goal of creating a legacy.

Protecting or Establishing an Estate: Similarly, life insurance can be used to protect or establish an estate. Some people may be concerned that the taxation on their final estate will be substantial and would like to have those funds lost to taxation replaced through a tax-free payout from an insurance policy. Others may feel that they really don't have an estate and would like to use insurance to create one.

An Alternative to Retirement Savings Accounts: This strategy, which is most commonly used by individuals in their forties and fifties who have put retirement savings on the back burner, helps to ensure that policy owners reach their retirement goals and objectives. Many people plan to retire around the same time that their parents are likely to pass away. The way this strategy works is by taking out a life insurance policy on your parents, who may be in their sixties or seventies. You pay the life insurance premiums and own the life insurance policy. For example, you may be 48 years old with a parent who is 72. If that parent dies at 87, you will be 63 and you will receive a lump sum, tax-free amount to use for retirement. The benefit to you is that the payout is guaranteed (you just don't know when), and you are guaranteed a tax-free rate of return (you just can't know for certain what it will be).

Recent changes in the pricing of insurance policies for older individuals has made this option less attractive but it remains effective.

Sheltering Assets from Taxation and Reducing Your Lifetime Tax Bill: This strategy can be effective when used in the context of a comprehensive financial plan prepared to help you identify and understand how much of your money you may not be using. Here's how it works: once we've established that you will not run out of money and identify how much money you are likely to have left over, we can conservatively take half or a third of that amount and roll it into a permanent life insurance policy through annual premiums. So, instead of taking the extra $10,000 a year that you have and investing it in GICs or bonds or stocks (which may go up or down in value and will create taxable income), you take that same amount of money and put it into a permanent life insurance policy that is guaranteed to pay out tax-free outside of your estate. You add the person or persons you wish to receive the payout as named beneficiaries on the policy.

Sheltering Assets from Creditors: Both in whole life and universal life policies, the investment assets are not considered part of an individual's or a business's assets. As such, these insurance tools can be used to shelter assets from creditors in the event that you need to declare bankruptcy or are exposed to liability.

Life Insurance as an Asset Class

When you start to think about insurance as a financial tool and asset, you can start to incorporate it into your overall asset allocation and financial plan. If you have permanent insurance, the policy is guaranteed to pay out, so it makes sense to include it in your financial asset allocation.

A typical net worth asset allocation may look like this:

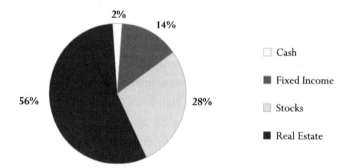

Adding insurance as an asset class increases your diversification and reduces your overall risk and exposure to one class. So your net worth asset allocation might now look something like this:

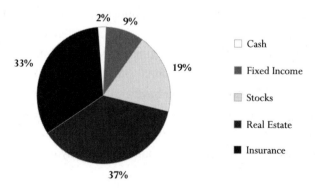

Cassandra and Alex

Cassandra and Alex, their three young children, and two dogs lived in one of the nicer parts of the Cathedral area in Regina. Alex worked at a local oil-and-gas company in middle management, and Cassandra worked part-time at one of the trendy cafés on 13th Avenue during the day while the kids were at school. Then, in 2005, Alex's company was taken over and his job was eliminated.

In the months that followed, Cassandra picked up as many shifts at the café as she could while Alex trained as a realtor, and they lived on his severance package. His entry to the field coincided perfectly with an unexpected surge in Saskatchewan's economy and a huge turnover in the real estate market, as long-time homeowners cashed in on skyrocketing prices and people flooded into Regina to take advantage of the boom.

In September 2007, Alex developed a pounding headache, which was unusual for him. By evening, he was having problems seeing and was feeling increasingly nauseated. Cassandra took him to emergency—busy as always—and they waited. Alex's condition worsened rapidly and, after waiting for several hours, he lost consciousness. When the nurses rushed over, they realized that Alex had stopped breathing. They began CPR and tried resuscitation, but it was too late. Cassandra was later told that the autopsy revealed a ruptured cerebral aneurysm.

Cassandra was devastated. The next few days were a blur as her in-laws arrived from Estevan to arrange to have the body shipped back home for the funeral. Her parents arrived and took her and the kids back home, and somehow Cassandra made it through the funeral and wake. Then reality started to sink in.

Not only had she lost her husband, she now had an entirely new financial reality to deal with. Alex had died with a will, but Cassandra quickly discovered he was seriously under-insured. She was certain that there was some type of insurance policy because she remembered him complaining about the deductions on his paycheque. She looked into it with the help of her lawyer, and they found that although Alex had had group life insurance at his old company, he had lost it when he lost the job. They hadn't been able to afford any insurance while Alex was unemployed and once he started making money at real estate, he had been too busy to deal with it. There was no life insurance coverage.

Going back through his bank statements, Cassandra discovered that he had critical illness insurance. She contacted the insurance company and filled out the claim form for the $100,000 policy but was informed that because Alex had not survived for 30 days after diagnosis, she was only entitled to a return of premiums. This amounted to just less than $3,600. Cassandra was beside herself. How could she support three kids and pay all the bills while working at a café?

She couldn't. Cassandra struggled through the next year with tremendous grief and financial stress. After watching her retirement savings disappear and her debt increase, she made a drastic decision. She sold the house in the summer of 2008 and moved back to Estevan until she could figure out what to do. She used the proceeds from the sale of the house to pay off her debt and create a small emergency savings account for herself and the kids.

Her parents took them in and proved to be excellent caregivers for the kids. Truth be told, both sets of grandparents were overjoyed to have their grandchildren so close to them, and the kids' sadness slowly began to lift in their new environment. As for Cassandra, now that she was back in her hometown, she benefited tremendously from the support of her family and friends and quickly found employment at a company that provides equipment to the oil industry. At this point, Cassandra contacted me to help her manage her finances and prepare a financial plan.

Cassandra and I recently had our annual check-up to review her financial plan, including her insurance coverage. She is rightfully proud of what she has accomplished in just a few short years. She and the kids are all adequately insured. Cassandra purchased a blended Term 20 and universal life policy to ensure she had sufficient coverage until the kids were about 25. She also wanted to make sure her kids would be able to have insurance protection and purchased small, inexpensive universal life policies for each of them that will create security for their families down the road. This past year she moved out of her parents' house and, with their help, bought her own house in the same subdivision—giving both her and her parents a little more space. She told me that three years ago she was sure she would never be happy again, but that she is now feeling hope return and is determined to give her kids the best future possible.

Charles and Tyson

Charles and Tyson have been together for 15 years and were among the first same-sex couples in British Columbia to get married when the law changed in the summer of 2003. Shortly after they were married, they adopted two children, who are now 6 and 7. Tyson is a partner at a large advertising firm in downtown Vancouver, while Charles runs a part-time concierge service and ensures that the home is well run.

They approached me recently about a gap in their financial planning. They had recently lost one of their best friends in a car accident, and they wanted to talk about life insurance. I explained that there are two types of insurance: the kind that helps you when you are living and the kind that takes care of your loved ones after you die. They quickly decided that they both wanted critical illness insurance to protect them while they were living, but the life insurance part took a bit longer.

We talked about the various life insurance options available, including term, whole life, and universal life insurance, and the possible combination of policies that would best suit them at this stage. I also explained how we could use income replacement or expense reduction calculations to determine how much insurance was needed. They decided to use income replacement as they had years ahead of raising the children and building their lives together, and they didn't want to lose their standard of living if something should happen to either one of them. Tyson makes approximately $250,000 per year including bonuses and, after his taxes and personal expenses (such as his car, parking, and other work and recreational expenses), contributes $115,000 to the home. Charles makes about $30,000 per year from his concierge business, which works out to around $13,000 after taxes and personal expenses. Based on these numbers, it seemed obvious to them that Tyson required far more insurance than Charles—at least in the short term.

This is when I pointed out something that the vast majority of couples forget: the value of the work done in the home. Tyson cheerfully admits that Charles is the "neat freak" and that without him the house would be a disaster, the bills would never be paid on time, and the kids would be dirty and hungry. So we calculated the amount of unpaid labour that would have to be replaced if anything should happen to him. Hiring a housekeeper, cook, or nanny, as well as a bookkeeper to deal with the finances, would add significant expenses. After we had completed the calculations, they agreed that they needed more insurance on Charles than simply enough to replace his income. This meant generating about $70,000 in income from an insurance payout of about $1.5 million for Charles and $100,000 from a payout of $2.25 million for Tyson, taking into account decreasing purchasing power caused by inflation.

They decided not to use whole life insurance because of its limitations, and, because the amount of insurance was sizeable, they didn't want to commit the entire amount to permanent universal life insurance. Additionally, we knew that their expenses would decrease once the kids left home and they paid off their mortgage. We decided that a blended life insurance package was the best choice for them, with 20-year term insurance for the bulk of the coverage, and a universal life policy to cover the insurance they wanted to have forever, both as a security net and as an investment vehicle.

During this process, Charles told me about the $50,000 permanent policy his parents had purchased for him when he was a child and asked if it would be a good idea for their children. I told him that it was always something to consider if the extra premium would not add too much financial stress. They decided to purchase $100,000 of permanent insurance for each of their children. We also changed the designated beneficiary on Charles' policy. To this point his beneficiaries had been his parents, but now it made more sense to designate Tyson. We'll talk more about designating beneficiaries in Chapter 11 because it can be an important estate-planning tool. Many people designate their estate as their primary beneficiary, but that is rarely the best strategy to reduce lifetime tax bills. We made sure that Charles and Tyson designated each other on their policies, with the kids as secondary beneficiaries through a trust.

Within a month, after the medical questionnaire and exams were completed, they were given clean bills of health and approved for their policies. They let me know how much better they felt knowing that everyone was now protected.

Chapter Summary

- Determine how much life insurance you need.
- Determine what you need it for—now and in the future.
- Determine the type of insurance you need—permanent or term.
- Work with an independent insurance broker to decide if you need:
    - Joint or individual policies.
    - Paid up or payable for life.
    - Return of premium.
- Think about insurance as an investment tool and asset class:
    - Do you want to create a guaranteed estate or legacy?
    - Should you insure a parent to help your retirement savings?
    - How can you use it to shelter money from taxation?
    - How can you reduce your investment risk by creating a guaranteed asset class?

How To Eat An Elephant.ca—Web Tools

Insurance Needs Analysis Tool

This tool will help you to determine whether you have too much, too little, or the right amount of insurance coverage. It is not meant to replace the advice of a competent independent insurance broker. Be sure to have on hand copies of any existing life insurance policies as well as any education savings account statements.

> **STEP ONE:** Log into www.howtoeatanelephant.ca and select the **Life Insurance Needs Analysis Tool** from the menu page.
>
> **STEP TWO:** Start by answering the series of questions for both you and your spouse. If you are unsure what you should fill in, simply click on the words in the sidebar dictionary to obtain an explanation for each of the fields.
>
> **STEP THREE:** If you answer yes to the question "Do you have existing life insurance?", fields will appear where you can enter the information about each policy. Select the type of policy, the number of years remaining, the premium amount and frequency that you pay that premium. Finally, enter the death benefit amount. When you have finished, click the **Save** button.
>
> **STEP FOUR:** When you are satisfied that you have entered all the information, click the **Get Report** button.
>
> **STEP FIVE:** Here you are presented with your report, which you can download and print as a PDF document.

I strongly encourage you to review this report and your personal financial situation with an independent insurance broker to help you determine which type of insurance and how much may be most appropriate for you.

PART
THREE

GROWING YOUR FINANCES

8

RETIREMENT AND ESTATE PLANNING

Don't simply retire from something; have something to retire to.
—Harry Emerson Fosdick

WHEN MOST PEOPLE THINK ABOUT retirement, they think about the end of something. The dictionary defines it as "the removal or withdrawal from service." When I work with clients to prepare their financial plans, retirement is always one of the biggest areas that people want to get greater insight into and information on. Many of them look at retirement as the end of something, and I encourage them to start looking at it as the start of what *they* want to do!

Over the years I've seen many people retire from work, and they tend to fall into one of three categories:

- Some retire and end up going back to work, sometimes as a consultant or an employee working for someone else, or maybe they even start their own company, but in essence they continue to work.
- Some know exactly what they want to do with their retirement. They have passions and activities and things to keep them busy. These things tend to fill up their time. They say to me, "I'm busier now than I've ever been. How did I ever find the time to work?"
- Some retire and, in essence, find a hammock or a couch, and watch TV. They don't really do a whole lot. They tend to suffer

from declining health and pass away earlier than if they had some passion, interest, or hobby to keep them occupied.

Often, in preparing a retirement plan, the hardest question to answer is not, "Do I have enough money?" but, "What do I want to do in retirement?"

It's easy for many financial people to tell you that you need to save thousands of dollars to have enough money to retire, but until you clearly define what it is you want to do, it is very difficult to determine exactly how much money you will need.

Several times, I've worked with people in preparing a financial plan and, when they tell me what it is that they want to do, they realize that in order to save that amount of money, they need to make substantial sacrifices now. In these cases, some choose to change their lifestyle now, and others choose to scale back their future plans.

And then there are those who give me a lifestyle goal to work with for their retirement needs and, through preparing a proper financial plan, we learn that they will end up with extra money based on their current investments and savings. I encourage these individuals to take a good look at what they're doing now and live their lives more for today, and consider living a larger lifestyle during retirement.

So step one to retirement planning is to determine what your retirement lifestyle will be and what it will cost. One of the best ways to do this is to revisit the goals list that you started back in Chapter 1 and add some retirement goals to your list.

As you continue to read through this chapter, I will help you to identify some of the changes that should be taking place as you prepare and move into retirement—things like lower taxes, changes in expenses, and how much you spend as you age. I'll help you to identify where all your sources of income are going to come from to help you understand the various types of retirement savings programs and introduce you to some you may never have heard of.

Retirement Savings Options

Let's take a look at some of the more common retirement savings options you may be aware of.

Registered Retirement Savings Plans (RRSPs)

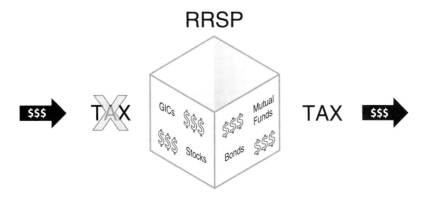

The easiest way for me to describe what an RRSP is, is to say that it's like a box—a holding place to put investments such as GICs, stocks, bonds, or mutual funds. Now, there are rules for what happens when you put investments into the box and there are rules about how you take things out of the box. So, an RRSP really isn't anything: it's simply a place to store investments, generally for retirement.

Keeping things in simple terms, the government will allow you to put up to 18% of your income into the box, to a maximum (in 2012) of $22,970. This amount can be deducted from your income for the year. When you put money and/or investments into your RRSP box, the government says you don't have to pay tax on income equivalent to the amount that you put into your RRSP. So, if you earned $100,000 and you put $10,000 worth of cash and investments into your RRSP box and claimed that on your income tax return, the government would say you only earned $90,000.

If you already paid tax on that $100,000, then the government would need to refund you approximately 41 cents for every dollar you put into your RRSP. So, if you put $10,000 into your RRSP, you could expect to get a refund of approximately $4,100. If you earn $45,000 a year, you can expect to get back approximately 26 cents for every dollar you put into your RRSP.

As long as you keep your money in your RRSP box, the government allows it to grow tax-free. So if you can earn a good rate of return, you will see that money grow and you won't have to pay taxes on that growth.

Should you decide to take money out of your RRSP box at any given time, the government will require you to pay tax on that money as if it were income you had earned. (There are a few exceptions, such as withdrawing the money for the home buyers' plan, which helps first-time home buyers to purchase a house, as well as withdrawals made to help pay for recognized education.) So, if you earned $100,000 and instead decided to withdraw $10,000 from your RRSP box, you would be required to pay the government approximately $4,100 in income tax.

One Frank Thought

I want everyone to start thinking of RRSPs as tax deferral tools rather than retirement savings tools. What I mean by this is that if you are in a high-income job, I would encourage you to use RRSPs to shelter assets to reduce your taxes while you're in the high-income position. Should you decide to leave your high-income position (maybe to have a child, start your own business, or simply change jobs), take a look at your income level for the year and consider whether or not it makes sense to take money out of your RRSP box and pay the taxes on the withdrawal, because you will be in the lower tax bracket.

For example, you may be a young, successful woman in her early thirties making $150,000 a year, and you may plan to start a family in a year or two and take some time off. While you are making a high income, you could put aside maybe $20,000 a year into your RRSP and get about 45 cents on the dollar back from making that contribution. Then, when you take a year or more off to have a child, you could consider withdrawing the money out of your RRSP and generating income of maybe $20-$30,000 a year. In this situation, you would only have to pay the government approximately 25 cents on every dollar withdrawn from your RRSP.

So, in essence, you have deferred your income from a high-tax year to a low-tax year and in doing so have saved yourself 20 cents on the dollar in taxes. Or, in the case of a $20,000 contribution and withdrawal, you've saved yourself nearly *$4,000* in taxes.

In order to effectively use your RRSP, you need to take into consideration what your income will be during your working years, and then assess what the withdrawals will be from your RRSPs in your retirement and your estate years. This will be one of the biggest factors determining whether or not you should be contributing money to an RRSP or to one of the other retirement savings programs, such as a tax-free savings account, or TFSA. Be sure to go onto the website and use the RRSP or TFSA calculator to help you determine whether it makes more sense to contribute money to one program or the other.

Tax-Free Savings Accounts (TFSAs)

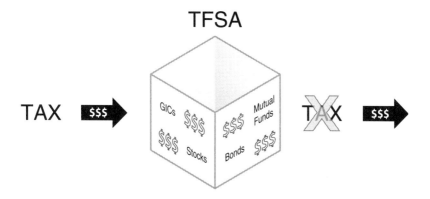

Sticking with the RRSP box analogy, tax-free savings accounts are another type of box that has its own rules. The rules for this box are:

- You can currently put up to $5,000 in the box each year.
- While the money is invested inside that box, it is allowed to grow tax-free.
- When you choose to withdraw the money from that box, there is no tax owing.

The biggest con to the TFSA is that you do not receive any sort of tax deduction from the contribution to this program. As well, the amount you're allowed to contribute is typically less than what you are allowed to contribute to an RRSP.

The pros of the TFSA box are that money grows tax-free while it's inside the box, and upon withdrawal you do not have to pay any tax on the money. This not only becomes a very powerful tax-planning income tool in retirement but also an effective estate-transitioning tool for estate planning. Another benefit is that you never lose the contribution room—any withdrawals get added back to your future contribution room the next year!

RRSP or TFSA?

This debate comes down to your annual tax rate in any given year and your tax rate in future retirement years. When you deposit money into an RRSP you get a tax deduction, but when you start withdrawing the money you have to pay tax on it. So if your income is much higher today than it will be in retirement, then contribute to your RRSP. If your income will be high both today and in retirement, then contribute to both an RRSP and a TFSA. If your income is low today and will be high in retirement, contribute to a TFSA. If your income is low today and will be low in retirement, contribute to a TFSA.

RRSP or TFSA?		**Retirement Income**	
		High	*Low*
Working Income	*High*	Both	RRSP
	Low	TFSA	TFSA

Company Pension Plans

Company pension plans can be a great way to save money on a regular basis. As we discussed in Chapter 5, these pension plans, whether funded by the employee or through the employer, can help you to save significant amounts of money in a registered plan. Many people find it difficult to save without a forced savings plan. Being part of a company pension plan and having contributions automatically deducted from their paycheques helps people to learn how to get by on less while saving for their later years. Whether it is a defined contribution plan (where you know how much you have to put into the plan), a defined benefit plan (where you know how much you will receive out of the plan), or a group RRSP plan (where you choose how much to contribute), the pension plan will result in greater savings than you might otherwise have and help you have a better quality of life in retirement.

Savings

Depending on your situation, you may have been able to accumulate money in a non-registered investment savings account or maybe even a simple bank account. The pros of having this savings box are that you can deposit and withdraw money from it at any time without restrictions being imposed by the government. One of the big cons of this box is that you receive no tax deductibility for deposits and any growth in accumulation of the money within that box is taxable. In Chapter 10 we will discuss how to properly invest within a savings box to minimize the tax liability from the growth of the investments.

In retirement, the savings box can be very helpful in providing income without incurring a higher level of taxable income. What I mean by this is that if you have $40,000 in taxable income—maybe from a pension or an RRSP or from the work that you're doing—you can supplement that $40,000 with an additional $10,000, $20,000, or even $30,000 from your savings box with only a minor amount of additional taxation. (The taxation usually comes from capital gains when you sell investments that are inside your savings box.)

The Forgotten Sources of Retirement Income

Many people wander around trying to figure out how much money they need to save for retirement. They forget about all the money that they've contributed toward the government programs. The Canada Pension Plan (CPP) and the Old Age Security (OAS), when combined, can make up a good portion of a retiree's income. This may mean $18,000 a year for an individual or possibly $36,000 or more for a couple (based on 2012 payment rates).

**	Individual	Couple
CPP	$10,000	$7,000
OAS	$6,000	$6,000
Total	$16,000	$13,000

$29,000

**Example using approximate averages for a two-income family.

Canada Pension Plan

This is a pension. Many people don't think of it this way: that they are contributing from every single paycheque to the Canada Pension Plan. Many people think of it as a tax, but in reality what you are doing is saving for your retirement. In 2011, changes to the CPP made it less attractive to take it early and more attractive to delay taking it. This change was likely due to the government's recognition that many baby boomers are applying early for their CPP benefits and worry that this may create a substantial drain on the CPP, thereby putting it in jeopardy.

Here is a brief explanation of the changes to the pension payouts: in 2011 CPP pensions were reduced by 6% for each year benefits were started prior to the age of 65, to a maximum of 30%. A larger reduction factor will be phased in during the period 2012–2016, after which pensions will be reduced by 7.2% a year for each year they are started early, to a maximum of 36%.

CPP pensions were increased in 2011 by 6.84% for each year they are started later than the regular retirement age of 65, to a maximum of 34.2%. A larger increase won't be phased in until 2013, when pensions will be increased by 8.4% a year for each year they are started later, to a maximum of 42%.

Under the new rules, if you live an average lifespan, you'll get the biggest lifetime payout by waiting until age 70 to begin drawing on CPP. The government has increased the penalty for taking CPP early across the board, so you'll get a smaller lifetime payout by taking it early, however long you live.

As a general rule, though, if you think you'll die young, take CPP early. If you think you'll live to be 93, put it off as long as you can.

One Frank Thought

My personal belief is that you would be smart to get the money while you can. Governments change these rules regularly, and you never know what's going to happen down the road. By getting the money early, you can enhance your quality of life now, while you're young and still able to go out and enjoy it. As you get into your later years, you tend to slow down and not need as much income. The only time I would wait is if you still have a very high income, as more than 40% of your CPP will just end up being repaid to the government in the form of taxes.

Old Age Security

This is not a pension. Old Age Security is a social security welfare program, funded out of general tax revenues, to help seniors increase their quality of life. It is designed to support those who have a lower income. If you have a much higher income, you will have your OAS reduced and/or completely eliminated. If your taxable income rises above $69,562 (2012), you will see your Old Age Security reduced by 15 cents for every dollar of additional income. So, if you earned an additional $10,000 of taxable income above the $69,562 limit, you would see approximately $1,500 of your Old Age Security clawed back. The maximum Old Age Security benefit for 2012 was $6,418.

In order to qualify for Old Age Security, you must be at least 65 years of age, you must live in Canada and be a Canadian citizen or legal resident, and you must have lived in Canada for at least 10 years after turning 18 years of age.

Or, if you live outside of Canada, you must be at least 65 years of age, you must have been a Canadian citizen or legal resident of Canada before having left Canada, and you must have lived in Canada for at least 20 years after turning 18.

To receive full OAS, you have to have lived in Canada for at least 40 years after turning 18. If you did not live in Canada for 40 years after turning 18, you can still qualify for partial Old Age Security. To calculate how much you would qualify for, simply divide the number of years you were in Canada after turning 18 by 40. For example, had you been in the country for 10 years after turning 18, you would qualify for 10 divided by 40—or one quarter—of the full amount.

Both OAS and CPP are indexed to the government's consumer price index to help protect you against inflation. Both OAS and CPP are taxable sources of income.

One Frank Thought

At the time of writing, the government passed legislation that changes the age at which Canadians qualify for OAS from 65 to 67 for those born after March 1958. For the majority of Canadians this will have a very minimal impact on their overall retirement plans. Simply put, if you were born after March 1958, you will have to wait until you are 67 to start collecting your OAS. This means you will lose the equivalent of approximately $13,000 (in 2012 dollars). This small loss should not be enough to derail your retirement plans (especially if you are following this guide).

Retirement Savings Options You May Not Have Heard Of

Depending on their age and stage of life, some people are left with very little time and or very little money to meet their retirement goals. With the high cost of real estate in Canada, many are being stretched beyond their means and have no way to put aside a little extra for retirement. Others don't make retirement a priority and find themselves less than 10–15 years away from retirement wondering how they will ever save enough to have a good lifestyle after leaving the workforce. Here are a few ways you may be able to find the funds necessary to have a better quality of life in retirement.

Real Estate

For the past 10 years there's been an ongoing debate as to whether or not there is a real estate bubble in Canada. This debate has been fuelled by the collapse of the real estate market in the United States and its failure to recover. For nearly 70% of Canadians, home ownership remains a fundamental priority. Given this very high ratio, real estate becomes a very real asset for most Canadians. The goal of many Canadians is to be mortgage-free when they retire. In some cases, this results in the retiree being house-rich but cash-poor. In order for them to find the funding to pay for their retirement, they may need to use the equity in their house to generate the necessary income.

There are several ways to generate this income. It can be through downsizing the house and taking the extra cash, investing it, and spending it. The retirees could sell the house and start renting a place, although by doing this, they create an additional expense requiring them to generate even more money for their retirement lifestyle. They also could look to borrow money from the house and use it to invest and generate income on a regular basis.

Each retiree will have their own preference as to which option to choose. These decisions should be made in the context of a comprehensive financial plan to help them to determine which scenario makes sense in relation to their goals.

Purchasing Life Insurance

Many people who are trying to determine how they're going to save sufficient money for retirement may want to look at life insurance policies as an option. What makes this option unique is that you would be taking life insurance out on your parent. Now, for many this may sound morbid, but it is a sound investment, and an effective tax- and retirement-planning strategy. I do not want you to wish your parents ill; I only want you to look at the various options that may exist to help to generate the retirement savings you need.

Here's how this works: let's say you are 45 years old and your mother is 70. If we assume your mother will live a long, healthy life, it is expected that she will pass away at the age of 87. When she passes, you will be approximately 62 years old. This is about the time that most people plan to retire. So, provided mom is in relatively good health, you look to take out a $500,000 life insurance policy on her and pay the premiums of $17,200 a year. So, in the 17 years in which you contribute to the insurance policy to fund your retirement plan, you end up paying a total of $292,400 (17 × $17,200). When your mom passes, you will receive a tax-free, lump sum payout of $500,000 from the life insurance policy, which you can use to fund and invest for your retirement.

The pros to this are that the half-million dollars are paid out tax-free. The growth of your money is tax-free and no matter how long mom lives, you're guaranteed a rate of return. Without knowing when mom may pass, we cannot calculate the exact rate of return. (In the example given, the rate of return is approximately 5.7% a year after tax. Which, if you have a 40% tax rate, is the equivalent of buying a 7.5% GIC.)

Some of the other advantages include the fact that you don't need to worry about the volatility of the stock market when investing your $17,200 a year in the policy and, when set up properly, the policy is creditor-proof.

The cons of this program are that you have to have someone you can insure; usually it's a parent. Your parent needs to be in relatively good health, and you need to get their permission to insure them. The biggest problem with this type of retirement savings is that you never know when you will be receiving the funds. You do know that you will receive the funds, you just don't know when.

One Frank Thought

Remember that this should only be used as part of your retirement plan. Should the insured live a long life, the funds can be used for retirement income in the later part of retirement and your other savings can be used up first.

That's the list of eight different options for retirement savings. We looked at RRSPs, TFSAs, company pensions, non-registered savings accounts, Canada Pension Plan, Old Age Security, real estate, and life insurance. A good combination of these options will help to ensure you have sufficient funds for retirement. So now let's take a look at income in retirement.

Will I Outlive My Money?

This is probably one of the biggest questions asked when people come to me to have a financial plan prepared. Understandably, worry about not having money or running out of money can be a major stress factor. Getting this one simple question answered can help to alleviate a lot of that anxiety and lead to improving your quality of life, both now and in the future. So let's get this question answered!

If you've done the exercises in the previous chapters, you've already done most of the work necessary to determine whether or not you will outlive your money. Where most mistakes are made is in determining how much money you will require to support the lifestyle you desire in retirement. Many people simply pick a number out of the air—such as $100,000 a year. Many financial resources will tell you that you need to have 70% of your pre-retirement income to cover your retirement lifestyle expenses.

One Frank Thought

I have a real problem with the 70% of pre-retirement income number. Everybody will have a different type of retirement in mind. Retirement income should not be based on pre-retirement income but on retirement expenses! Many people may not need to save anything beyond what their pension will provide because their pension will pay them more than they are likely to spend in retirement. Others may have lavish plans and goals for retirement, which may include purchasing a property in a warmer climate or buying an expensive yacht and spending their time sailing. Others may wish to join expensive golf clubs and country clubs, and they may require much more income post-retirement than they did pre-retirement. That's why I believe it's critical that each person take the time to determine what their lifestyle plans are and do a little research to determine what the cost of that lifestyle may be in retirement. As you continue reading, I will walk you through some of the things to be thinking about and looking at when determining your retirement income needs.

The best way to get a good understanding of and handle on costs and needs in retirement is through the preparation of a proper, comprehensive financial plan. You've heard me say this time and time again throughout this book, but it is this type of planning that helps you to discover where you truly stand and gives you a good estimate of your financial situation going forward for the rest of your life.

Sources of Income in Retirement

Many people look at their pension statements or their RRSP savings and think there is insufficient money there to enable them to retire. Many times, I've sat down with people who come to me looking for some help and answers, and they say, "I'm currently making $5,000 a month and just getting by; how am I going to live on my $2,400-a-month pension?"

As I start to ask them questions and go through their financial situation, I show them that there are seven different sources of retirement income in addition to a pension. Let's take a look at a few of these options:

- CPP, as mentioned above, could add up to $11,000 a year in income.
- Old Age Security could give you another $6,000 a year in income.
- If you have money saved in an RRSP, it might generate another $5,000–$10,000 a year in income, or maybe even more.
- The new tax-free savings accounts can provide some tax-free income throughout your retirement.
- Non-registered savings accounts will provide some income, if you've been able to set aside a little bit of your $5,000-a-month paycheque for a rainy day.
- Inheritance. Many people don't think about it, but I frequently run into people who say, "I just inherited a couple of hundred thousand dollars." People often don't wish to include this in their planning, but it is definitely a source of assets that may help in funding retirement income.
- Other sources include real estate through a reverse mortgage, downsizing, or selling your property off completely.

All of these, when added to your $2,400-a-month pension, may be more than sufficient to cover your retirement lifestyle.

Let's take a look at John and Mary. They are 65 and 66 years old respectively. Both are now retired after having worked for many years. Mary took 10 years off to raise the children, who have now moved out of the house. They determine that for them to be able to live comfortably in retirement they need approximately $60,000 a year in after-tax money.

John has a pension from his work that pays him a total of $32,000 a year before tax, and he has a total of $15,000 in RRSP savings. He does not expect to receive any inheritance as he has four siblings and an ailing mother. Mary has no pension but has accumulated $123,000 in her RRSP and expects to receive about $50,000 in inheritance. They have a house worth approximately $330,000 that is mortgage-free and have joint savings totalling approximately $40,000. John and Mary can expect to receive nearly $32,000 a year from CPP and OAS combined. (CPP: John $11,520, Mary $8,280. OAS: John $6,000, Mary $6,000.)

When you combine the income from John's pension ($32,000) and the CPP and OAS payments, their total taxable income equals approximately $64,000 a year. Through income-splitting, the total amount of tax payable will be approximately $5,300 each, leaving them a net income of $53,400. What this means is that they only need to come up with an additional $6,600 a year in after-tax income to meet their lifestyle needs.

Given John and Mary's numbers, it is unlikely that they will outlive their money, and they're likely to leave an inheritance of approximately $1.2 million.*

How Is It That I Could Earn So Little and End Up with Enough Money for Retirement?

There are three major factors that change once you move from your working years into your retirement years. Although these don't apply to everyone, they seem to be a recurring theme in the planning work I do.

> **Lower tax rates:** In your retirement years, you tend to have less income, which means that you pay a lower tax rate. Many people also

---

* This is an after-tax, after-probate value, based on actuaria llife expectancy and Ontario tax rates.

derive income through Canadian dividend shares, which are very
tax preferred in comparison to interest or employment income.
If you are married or in a common-law relationship, you have the
opportunity to elect to split income between you and your partner.
This allows you to lower your taxable income even further by having
the total income between the two of you taxed almost evenly rather
than one spouse being taxed at a very high rate and the other at
a much lower rate. This can dramatically reduce the amount of
income required to generate the equivalent after-tax income.

Lower expenses: For many people, living expenses, once they reach
retirement, are typically lower: the kids have moved out of the house
and are financially independent, the mortgage is substantially paid
down or paid off, and most other debts have been paid down or
out. Of course, a lot of people have visions and plans for retirement
that include travelling and/or lifestyle needs that are much more
expensive than when they were working. It's not uncommon, for
example, for people to buy or rent properties in a warmer climate,
boats, RVs, or other retirement lifestyle assets.

Spending less with age: After years of financial planning, I've
learned that as people age they tend to slow down and not spend
as much as they did in the early years of retirement. When people
are 60 to 70 years old, they tend to be a lot more active than when
they're 70 to 80, and the trend grows more pronounced with the
passing years. Another thing I've noticed is that people tend to
start focusing more on family as they get into the later stages of
retirement. One factor influencing the change, I believe, tends to be
grandchildren and growing families, but there also is the desire to
spend time with those who matter most to them rather than flying
around the world on lavish vacations. Although the calculation is
not based on science, I typically look to reduce annual spending
by between 15 and 20% at around age 75, and by another 15 to
20% at around age 85. Because of these reductions in spending,
people don't need to save nearly as much money as they think they
need to.

One Frank Thought

It is only through preparing a comprehensive financial plan that you can see how all these variables—sources of income, overall tax rates, changes in expenses, and changes in spending—truly affect your overall financial life and how much you need to save for retirement. You may not believe this, but more often than not I meet people who have too much money saved for retirement, and I work with them to increase their quality of life now, and then help them to make wise decisions about giving assets to family and charities as part of their estate planning.

Retirement does not need to mean the end of something. It can mean the start of doing what you truly enjoy doing, and the freedom to choose your own path. Whether your goal is to engage in recreational activities, start your own business, spend time with family and friends, or simply relax at home, you will find that retirement is an opportunity!

Estate Planning

Most of us don't even start thinking about estate planning until we're well into our retirement years. It may be an illness or an accident that gets us to start thinking about our own mortality and what we need to do to prepare for our death. The earlier we start doing estate planning, the more options are available to us to substantially decrease our lifetime tax bill and increase our estate and quality of life.

The big problem with estate planning, though, is that many of us can't even understand or foresee the next year or five years, let alone start planning for 10, 15, 20, 30, or 40 years down the road. Once again, this is where preparing a comprehensive financial plan, using conservative estimates and realistic forecasts, can help to give you a rough idea of what your estate may look like down the road. Knowing and understanding what your estate situation may be can help you to make decisions today about increasing your quality of life and to make better life decisions going forward.

If, through preparing a financial plan, you learn that the likelihood is you will end up leaving an estate of a couple of million dollars, you may decide to spend more money now and/or start to give it to your children earlier. Too many times I have met people who have scrimped and saved throughout their entire retirement, trying to make sure that they don't out-live their money, and then they end up leaving $1 million or more to their estate. Their beneficiaries, most often their children, will remark that they would have preferred that their parents had spent the money and enjoyed their life rather than them ending up with a lot of money that they may or may not need.

The other outcome that can be revealed through proper financial planning is the amount of tax a person is likely to pay throughout their lifetime. In many cases, because the money is simply kept in investment accounts, it attracts a lot of taxation through interest income, dividends, and capital gains. By doing the proper financial plan and addressing estate planning, there are several strategies that can be used to reduce your lifetime tax bill.

Let's take a look at some of the ways to shelter your estate and reduce your lifetime tax bill.

Spend It!

One of the simplest and easiest solutions is to spend more money. That being said, for those who have saved for most of their lives, changing their spending habits can be a real challenge. Increasing your quality of life by making your goals a reality—taking those dream vacations, buying that dream boat/car, and so on—can help to reduce your savings and your estate, thereby reducing your taxable income and assets. The big trick here is not to spend too much! But by spending your money, you reduce the amount that you have saved and invested that is generating taxable income; this should reduce your lifetime tax bill.

One Frank Thought

Some may argue that by spending it, we end up having to pay sales tax on a number of items and, therefore, still end up with a significant tax bill.

Give It Away

Maybe you wish to help a family member accomplish some of their goals; maybe it's a neighbour, a friend, or a colleague. Knowing and understanding whether or not you have an excess of funds will empower you to make decisions to help others. Again, be sure not to give too much away because it's very difficult to get people to give it back!

Pay Down Your Children's Mortgages

The growth in value of a child's principal residence is a tax-free growth. If you intend to give your child this money anyway after you've passed, paying down his or her mortgage can be a way to take money that you are not going to be spending and investing it in a tax-sheltered investment. At the same time, this helps to alleviate some of the burden that your child may have taken on due to the high cost of housing these days.

One Frank Thought

You would be wise to take a promissory note from your child when you do this. In the event that your child's marriage ends, you can take back the money and give it to him or her once the divorce is finalized.

Fund Your Children's Tax-Free Savings Accounts

This is another option where, if you plan to give money to your children anyway, you may be able to use the room in their tax-free savings accounts to deposit and shelter investment assets from taxation. In many cases, your children, under the strains of family obligations, may not be able to contribute to their tax-free savings accounts, giving you an opportunity to shelter investment assets and grow them tax-free to be inherited down the road. The big issue with this option is that you give up control of the investment assets as the TFSA accounts belong to your children. This means that at any time they are free to withdraw that money and use it as they see fit. Although this is a risk, many parents can have reasonable conversations with their children to explain that this is what they're doing and that the money is earmarked for them, provided Mom and Dad no longer need it.

Buy a Life Insurance Policy to Reduce Your Lifetime Tax Bill

If, by preparing a comprehensive financial plan, you discover that you may be leaving substantial assets as an estate, you may consider purchasing a permanent life insurance policy to not only reduce your lifetime tax bill but also to grow your overall estate. Rather than taking $20,000 a year and putting it into an investment account, which generates interest, dividends, and capital gains taxes, you take the same $20,000 and invest it in a permanent life insurance policy, which guarantees to pay out $750,000 at death. So, over a 20-year period, you may end up paying $400,000 into the policy rather than into an investment account. This $400,000 will grow to $750,000* tax-free and, if done properly, can also be protected against creditors.

Donate to a Recognized Charity

Charitable giving has many great benefits and rewards. Not the least of these benefits are substantial tax credits. When thinking about donating to charity, you should plan to take a strategic approach derived from a comprehensive financial plan. Let's take a look at a few of the more common ways to effectively donate to charity to reduce your lifetime tax bill.

> **Donate Shares and Land:** By donating assets, such as shares or real estate, that have appreciated and carry a capital gain, you not only receive the fair market value of the asset on your donation tax receipt, you also don't incur capital gains tax on the appreciation of that asset. For example, if you own shares in a public or private company that you purchased for $1,000 and they are now worth $10,000, you could donate them to charity and receive a charitable donation tax receipt for $10,000, and you do not need to pay capital gains tax on the $9,000 gain. The same is true with real property. Let's say you purchased some land many years ago for $5,000 and you wish to donate it to the Land Preservation Society. The property is currently worth $50,000. The Land Preservation Society would give you a charitable tax receipt for $50,000 and you would not have to pay capital gains tax on the $45,000 gain.

---

*The numbers above are for illustration purposes only. In addition to the tax savings, your $20,000-a-year investment isn't subject to the ups and downs of the market and can be quickly and easily distributed to your beneficiaries outside of your estate, tax- and probate-free.

Name a Registered Charity as a Beneficiary: By naming a charity as a beneficiary of a life insurance policy, trust, or registered account, the value of that account at death becomes a charitable donation and generates a tax credit of up to 100% of the value of your income in the year of death; this can also be carried back against your income in the previous year. In the case of life insurance policies, you may be able to claim the annual premium you pay as a charitable donation and use that tax credit every year until death.

Invest Assets and Donor-Advised Funds for Charitable Remainder Trusts: Although these aren't new, they are a rarely used way of making regular charitable donations over a number of years while still controlling the asset. The way these work is that you deposit money into a donor-advised fund or charitable remainder trust and it is invested. You do not pay any capital gains, interest, or dividend income on the investment income, and you can then designate to distribute X amount of dollars out of the trust or fund to the charity of your choice and receive a charitable tax receipt for the amount donated. These funds typically require you to donate a minimum percentage of the value of the fund each and every year. This typically is somewhere around 5%, so if the fund returns 10% or more, you can donate more, but you are still required to donate a minimum of 5%. Should you decide to collapse the fund at a future date and retain the assets from the fund, you may incur a tax liability at that time.

Probate

Probate is the legal process by which the courts recognize an individual's will as their official will. It is typically required after an individual has passed away and before estate assets can be distributed to the beneficiaries. Probate of a will is usually not required when all the assets pass from one spouse to another. Many institutions and estate trustees require a probated will to protect them against liability and claims from individuals stating that they were not authorized to distribute estate assets because the terms of the will are invalid. Having the courts officially recognize the will through the process of probate helps protect those individuals and companies against such claims and liabilities.

How Much Does Probate Cost?

Each province and territory has its own probate schedule. Where the trustee resides and where the estate assets reside will determine which jurisdiction will undertake probate. Some jurisdictions charge a flat fee, based on the amount of assets, and others charge a percentage of assets.

Let's look at a few ways to minimize or eliminate probate fees:

Gift Assets Prior to Death: Gift as many of your assets that you no longer need to the beneficiaries that you wish to have them. Doing this minimizes the value of your estate and thereby reduces the overall cost of probate. It also ensures that the beneficiary receives the asset in a timely manner.

Named Beneficiary: The simple act of naming beneficiaries on life insurance policies and investment accounts allows those assets to pass to the beneficiaries directly outside of your estate and, therefore, they are not subject to probate fees. Although a very effective method, this can create an uneven distribution of assets among your beneficiaries. For example, you could have an RRSP with a value of $100,000 and a non-registered investment account with a value of $100,000, and you could leave one to each of your children. The RRSP account will be subject to full taxation and minimum withholding taxes of up to 30% of its value before it will be transferred to your child. The non-registered account, however, won't lose any of its value and may leave a tax liability to the estate. As life insurance policies pay out tax-free, these can be very effective ways to distribute assets equally to your children.

Registering Assets in Joint Tenancy: Registering assets in joint tenancy with the individual whom you wish to receive those assets will see the assets transfer directly to them upon your death without ever having to pass through your estate or be subject to probate. In doing this, all owners of the joint tenancy are subject to their proportional ownership income taxation. So, if two people hold investment assets in joint tenancy and they generate $1,000 in income, each owner will have to declare $500 of income on their tax return.

There are several more advanced ways of transferring your estate and its value to future generations that can provide significant tax benefits. Using spousal or remainder trusts, or a holding corporation, can freeze the value of your estate, substantially reduce or spread the tax liability, and eliminate probate. As these are very complex estate planning and estate-freezing strategies, it is not wise to proceed without the guidance of a certified financial planner, estate lawyer, and tax accountant.

One Frank Thought

It is always valuable to weigh the cost and additional work involved when you are determining which option is best for the transition of your estate. You should never do this without first having a comprehensive financial plan prepared to help you understand the implications of the various options and their impact on your overall financial success.

Alejandro and Lucia

I've been working with Alejandro and Lucia since 2008, when a client referred them to me. They were in their early sixties; neither of them had a company pension, but they had just retired with sizeable RRSPs. They had never been big spenders and had made it one of their goals to set aside money throughout their working lives. At the beginning of 2008, they had a combined RRSP value of $1.3 million. This was safely over the $1.2 million that Alejandro had decided was their number, the amount of money they felt they *had* to have to feel secure enough to retire. I have discovered that the number is one of the most flawed concepts in financial planning. Almost everyone has a special number that, in his or her mind, equates to financial security. But very few people base their number on a comprehensive financial plan. Often, they pick a number out of the air or play around with inadequate calculators online, or listen to some financial product salesperson.

When Alejandro first contacted me in March 2008, their portfolio had just dropped in value from $1.3 to $1.1 million in the January stock market correction. He was preparing to go back to work, convinced that they did not have enough money for retirement. I asked him to send me their investment statements, which showed mostly mutual funds, and I was shocked to see that it contained 75% equity funds! At 63? I couldn't believe it. I asked him why they had a 45-year-old's portfolio, and his reply was that's what they always had done. I told him that they needed to take some risk off the table. Right now.

One Frank Thought

At age 63 you should not have that much of your retirement savings in equities. Sadly, this is a fairly common problem: people don't change how they invest. When they're 65, they think they're 40, and they don't think about their risk. As people near retirement, they need to be more conservative and build a portfolio focused on asset preservation and income generation rather than growth.

As the stock market began to recover through the spring and early summer, I prepared their comprehensive financial plan to determine how much money they really needed and where their money would be best protected. Unfortunately, I still did not have 100% buy-in from them, and they did not act quickly on my recommendations.

At the end of the summer, Alejandro went back to work, and the stock market began its quick slide from September through November. They did not put their new financial plan into effect until his portfolio had plummeted to $880,000. They were despondent when they came in for their meeting, and Lucia nearly wept as she explained that Alejandro would never be able to retire.

But that all changed as I began to explain that they were okay, and even with assets at this much lower level, the plan was going to work.

- They had no consumer debt, and they had paid off their mortgage.
- Alejandro wanted to keep his membership at the local golf club and play his three rounds per week.
- Lucia wanted money to spoil their many grandchildren.
- They wanted to spend lots of time with their family.
- They wanted to take the occasional vacation.

Their financial plan clearly showed that $65,000 per year after tax was more than enough to accomplish these goals. Including their CPP and OAS incomes and anticipating a conservative 6% return on their investments, they could more than fund their plan. In fact, they would still have enough, 30 years down the road, to leave $600,000 to their children. I could see Lucia and Alejandro visibly relax as I explained that he didn't need to go back to work and that everything was going to be fine.

They did have one more goal we needed to address: they wanted to leave a sizeable inheritance to their children and grandchildren when they passed on. Because of inflation, $600,000 today would only be worth $250,000 30 years from now. How could we increase their estate? The answer: life insurance.

I helped them arrange a joint last-to-die life insurance policy, with the help of their two children, that will increase their estate by $480,000. Each child now pays one-third of the premium, and Alejandro and Lucia pay the final third. The children are investing $300 per month toward their own retirement, and, with the return-of-premium rider we attached to the policy, in 30 years it will be worth over $750,000, tax-free to each of their children. This combined with the nearly $600,000 in remaining assets will help them achieve their goal of leaving a sizeable estate.

I love using the example of Alejandro and Lucia because it clearly demonstrates that it is never too late for proper comprehensive financial planning. They now have peace of mind and a relaxing, joyful retirement with decreased taxes, increased after-tax income, and a better quality of life.

Max and Manon

Max and Manon run a successful adventure company in Timmins. They laugh about it now, but when they started 15 years ago, it was almost too much for them, especially with young children. But that was then, they like to remind me, and this is now. In their mid-forties, with two boys about to start university, they are enjoying the fruits of their labour and wondering, "What's next?" They contacted me after Max landed a huge contract to run corporate retreats for an industry association.

There were a few other factors in their decision to seek financial advice. Manon's parents were ready to retire and discovering that with five children and only one income they had not saved enough to move down south, which was what they had always wanted. Their stress was affecting the whole family. Manon loved her parents but didn't want to end up like them. The other major factor was that Max's father had passed away suddenly from a heart attack, leaving a small inheritance to Max and his three sisters. Watching their parents encounter aging in such profound ways had turned their thoughts toward their own retirement, and their lack of planning.

Over the years I have learned that there is no point in figuring out the how of financial planning if you haven't figured out the why, and so, with new clients, I always prefer to start at the very beginning—with goals. I provided Max and Manon with the goal-setting sheets from Chapter 1 and set an appointment in three weeks to go over their SMART goals.

As might be expected of a couple that runs an adventure company, their goals were rather . . . adventurous. They wanted to travel a lot, while at the same time keeping their home base in Timmins so that they could be close to family and friends. They wanted to retire at age 55, and they wanted to have a winter home near Hilton Head in South Carolina. Their business was running well and they wanted to set it up so that they could sell it in another 10 to 15 years.

After establishing their goals, with small steps to achieve each one, they developed a balance statement and budget. In most ways they were very responsible with their money, but we discovered two areas that were keeping them perpetually in the red. The first was their love of adventure travel, and the second was their boys' involvement in sports. We calculated that they were spending around $20,000 each year on rep hockey, baseball, basketball, and soccer, plus another $10,000 for their annual trip to an exotic location. They quickly realized, once they saw the numbers, that while their company was doing well, it wasn't doing well enough to support this lifestyle.

Happily, the combination of RESPs, scholarship money, and the money the boys earned at their summer jobs would more than pay for their school expenses, saving Max and Manon about $20,000 per year—not to mention the time that would be freed up. They also agreed to reduce their adventure vacations to one every two years, and to look for other adventures close to home the alternate year.

With increasing income, reduced expenses, and a new set of goals, we were ready to start looking at their savings options. After using the debt destruction calculator and creating an aggressive plan to reduce their consumer debt, they decided to accelerate payments on their mortgage. This would save them close to $30,000 in interest over the remaining 15 years of payments and ensure that they would be mortgage-free by the time they were 60. They really liked this idea because they were always hearing that mortgage rates were going to be going up. They wanted to pay down the mortgage while more of their payment was going against principal, before interest rates got high.

Max also invested most of his inheritance money into two TFSAs allocated between growth and income products. Since the inheritance was from a tax-free life insurance policy, we could save their RRSP contribution room for pre-tax money and capitalize on the tax-free growth of the TFSA. Finally, we arranged insurance for each of them and set up an automatic transfer each month from their chequing account to an RRSP to continue building their nest egg. When the financial plan was completed, they were happy to discover that they were well on their way to retiring with adequate resources to accomplish most of their goals, in the short and long term. While they may choose not retire at 55, they will be well on their way to an early retirement if they follow the plan.

Summary

- Revisit your goals from Chapter 1 and determine what you will do in retirement.
- Build a reasonable budget of what this will cost on an annual basis.
- Work with a certified financial planner (CFP) to build a comprehensive financial plan using conservative assumptions.
- Learn and understand all the different sources of income you will have in retirement.
- Work with your CFP to identify additional ways you can reduce your annual and lifetime tax bill.
- Once you have your plan and understand where all your income will come from and how much of an estate you will likely leave:
  ◦ Determine how you want to spend and distribute the money.
  ◦ Assess if you are comfortable taking the risks to achieve the returns.
  ◦ Recognize the various tax implications of the decisions you wish to make.
  ◦ Find ways you are comfortable with to deal with your assets.

How To Eat An Elephant.ca—Web Tools

Canadian Retirement Calculator

This calculator will help you to learn and understand whether you will or will not outlive your money and show you your various sources of retirement income. It will show you the difference between your current tax rate and your tax rate during retirement. You will also learn how much of an estate you are likely to leave.

This calculator is pre-populated with the information you provided in the Net Worth, Expenses, and Income Sources tools. If you have not already completed these tools, please go back and complete them before proceeding.

> **STEP ONE:** Log into www.howtoeatanelephant.ca and select the **Canadian Retirement Calculator** from the menu page.
>
> **STEP TWO:** Take a few minutes to review the information that appears in the various fields and ensure that it is correct. If there is incorrect information, you will need to correct it in the appropriate tool before returning to do this calculation.
>
> **STEP THREE:** Be sure to fill in any pension income that you will receive once retired. (Do not include CPP or OAS.) Enter your planned retirement age and whether or not you are a smoker. (Be sure that the gender is correct.) Do the same for your spouse.
>
> **STEP FOUR:** When you are satisfied that the information in the calculator is correct, click on the **Get Report** button.
>
> **STEP FIVE:** Here you are presented with your report, which you can download and print as a PDF document.

Remember that this tool is not meant to replace having a proper financial plan. A certified financial planner can prepare a comprehensive financial plan that will help you to save more money in taxes and give you the opportunity to enjoy a better quality of life.

Now let's find out if you should contribute to an RRSP or a TFSA account!

How To Eat An Elephant.ca—Web Tools

RRSP or TFSA Tool

This tool is used to help you determine whether you should be contributing money to an RRSP or to a TFSA, or possibly to both. It too is pre-populated with information from previous tools. Essentially, it compares your taxable income during your working years and your retirement years. It is very similar to the Canadian Retirement Calculator.

> **STEP ONE:** Log into www.howtoeatanelephant.ca and select the **RRSP or TFSA Tool** from the menu page.
> **STEP TWO:** Take a few minutes to review the information that appears in the various fields. If there is incorrect information, you will need to correct it in the appropriate tool before proceeding.
> **STEP THREE:** Be sure to fill in any pension income that you will receive once retired. (Do not include CPP or OAS.) Enter your planned retirement age and whether or not you are a smoker. (Be sure that the gender is correct.) Do the same for your spouse.
> **STEP FOUR:** When you are satisfied that the information in the calculator is correct, click on the **Get Report** button.
> **STEP FIVE:** Here you are presented with your report, which you can download and print as a PDF document.

Be sure to revisit this tool every year to help you determine whether you should be contributing your money to an RRSP or to a TFSA, or both. Remember this tool is not meant to replace proper planning. It is meant to give you guidance on where you should contribute. Be sure to sit down with a certified financial planner to help you prepare a financial plan that will show you definitively where to contribute your money.

9

INVESTING

That money talks I'll not deny,
I heard it once: it said, "Goodbye."

—*Richard Armour*

INVESTING CAN BE ONE OF the easiest areas of your finances, but for the majority of people it is the most confusing, mysterious, and stressful aspect of all. This is generally caused by the volume of products that are out there for people to invest their money in. Having so many different products to choose from tends to create confusion. One of the easiest ways to battle this confusion is by only focusing on the products that make the most sense for your financial situation.

> One of the best ways to reduce your investment risk and improve your overall return is to get an education!

Congratulations on making it this far! My guess is that fewer than 20% of the people who start this book will get this far. The fact that you have persevered shows that you have a desire to learn and take control of your finances. Let's keep going by looking at the myriad investment products that are available, understanding the relationship between risk and return, learning better ways to allocate your investments, and understanding basic rules of investing and diversification.

At the end I will share my thoughts on which products are the best to invest in for a given level of investable assets and what I believe is the best investment anyone can make.

Investment Products

Risk Rating

I have given a risk rating for each product to indicate the probability of you losing your money:

- **Very Low:** Not going to lose your money.
- **Low:** Very rarely will you lose money.
- **Medium:** You may lose money but likely not much.
- **High:** On any given day you could lose a notable amount of money.
- **Very High:** Very good chance you could lose money.
- **Extreme:** More often than not you will lose money.

Savings Accounts (Very Low): High-interest savings accounts have become a normal part of banking. These accounts typically pay a higher rate of interest than a regular bank account and can be a great tool for parking money on a short-term basis (from 30 days to six months). They are usually fully guaranteed and pay interest on a monthly basis. (Be careful about withdrawal fees and remember these are not transaction accounts.)

Guaranteed Investment Certificates (GICs) (Very Low): These certificates, typically issued by a bank, offer you a guaranteed investment at a set interest rate for a set period of time. Today, the rates on these certificates tend to be quite low and, once you factor in inflation and taxation, many of these certificates result in a loss in buying power. If the GIC pays 3%, you have to pay 1% of that to taxes, and if inflation is at 2.5%, you are actually losing 0.5% every year. There are very few times when GICs are the best option. Many times, the high-interest savings accounts offer competitive, if not better, rates in the short term (less than one year) and have the added flexibility of being available for withdrawal at any time.

Canada Savings Bonds (Very Low): Left over from the days of war bonds, Canada Savings Bonds offer the guarantee of the federal government but typically pay very low interest rates. To compound the problem, many of the current Canada Savings Bonds can be redeemed only once a year.

Government Bonds (Low): These are bonds that are issued by various governments (federal, provincial, and municipal) that typically pay a higher rate of interest than Canada Savings Bonds or GICs, and the investor has the option to buy and sell them most business days. These benefits of higher interest and greater flexibility in purchase and sale come with a slightly higher risk that you may lose some money.

How can you lose money by investing in bonds? Bonds, like many other assets, go up and down in price. Typically, based on $100 value when issued at a specific interest rate, this value can change either up or down depending on what the prevailing interest rates do. For example: if you buy a bond for $100 that is paying 5%, and then, a month later, a new bond equivalent to yours comes out and is paying 6%, your bond is no longer as valuable. So, if you want to sell your bond, you would have to reduce the price of it to make it more attractive for others to buy.

The reverse is also true: if a new bond equivalent to yours comes out and is paying only 4%, you could offer to sell your bond at a higher price because it's paying a higher rate of interest. So this is where you can have a gain or a loss when buying and selling bonds.

Corporate Bonds (Medium): These are issued when corporations borrow money from individual investors to fund ongoing operations. They have the same structure and set-up as government bonds, in that they have a term (such as one year, five years, 10 years, 25 years), and they have an interest rate that they pay for borrowing money from you. All bonds also have a credit rating. This is typically given by a third party that assesses the risk that the interest and/or principal of the bond may not be paid or repaid. Later in this chapter we'll talk about different types of risk, and credit risk will be explained in more detail.

As corporate bonds have a higher risk than government bonds, they also pay a higher rate of interest. They can be bought and sold on most business days.

Preferred Shares (Medium): These are shares in a business or corporation whose value doesn't typically go up or down too much. They tend to be issued at $25 each and usually have a set percentage dividend. For example, Bell Canada may issue a preferred share at $25 with a 5% dividend. This means that over the course of a year, Bell Canada will pay $1.25 per share in dividends. Sometimes the shares go up in value and sometimes they go down, but they don't generally move up or down a tremendous amount. Many people think of preferred shares as kind of a hybrid bond and stock because they don't have the volatility of the common share and they pay consistent dividends the way a bond would pay interest. Again, these shares can be bought and sold on most business days, and the dividend payment can be quite tax efficient.

Common Shares (High): These are shares in a corporation that are issued to raise money for business operations. They represent ownership in the company and may or may not pay a dividend. The shares tend to go up and down in value significantly more than other investments, such as bonds or preferred shares, and, therefore, carry higher risk. The shares can be classified as stocks, and many people will talk about "growth stocks" and "value stocks." Growth stocks are typically shares in a corporation that are unlikely to pay dividends, but are likely to significantly appreciate in value due to the growth of the company. Value stocks tend to be shares in a company that is well established and can generate a fair bit of cash and profit from ongoing business operations. Value stocks do not usually move up or down nearly as much as growth stocks, but they do tend to pay dividends more often. Typically, these shares can be bought and sold on any business day.

Private Placements (Very High): These are opportunities for individuals to invest (typically large sums of money) in a private company that does not have its stock listed on a public exchange. This is generally done with companies that are just starting out and may not have built their business up to a size that would warrant making a public offering of their shares. Although not always the case, private placements can be made with very large, successful companies that have decided not to become public companies.

The reason why the risk level on these investments is so high is because these companies do not need to disclose their financial records or comply with any regulatory body. As well, it can be very difficult to sell your shares in the company as there is no stock exchange or secondary market in which to find a buyer. These tend to be appropriate only for those people with very large investment assets.

Partnerships (Extreme): These are also opportunities for individuals to invest in private companies, this time by becoming a partner of the company through purchasing a minimum 10% of its value. They're very much the same as private placements, although they tend to have different purchase agreements and often require a much larger investment. In some instances the investor may be required to participate in the growth and ongoing operations of the business. Generally, if you wish to sell your shares, there are restrictions on who you can sell to and how and when you can sell them. Given these restrictions, it can be very difficult to get your money back and, therefore, the risk in these situations can be extreme.

Alternative Hybrid Investments

These investments are usually derived from other investments or are a combination of other products. Many attempt to decrease the risk and/or increase the return by modifying the structure of existing products.

Market-Linked GICs (Very Low): These are GICs that do not have a guaranteed interest payment. The company issuing the GIC (typically a bank) will pay interest based on the rate of return of a particular stock market. For example, if the Toronto stock market goes up 8% in one year, then your GIC will pay you 8%. If the Toronto stock market goes down during the year, the GIC will pay you 0%. Typically, the amount of interest you can earn is capped at a certain amount, maybe 10 or 12%, but your principal investment is guaranteed. In this situation, the risk you run is not making any money on your investments and actually losing money due to inflation.

Convertible Debentures (High): Don't let the fancy name of these investments confuse you. Convertible debentures are bonds that have a special feature that allows you to convert them into common shares. So you may purchase a bond that pays 5% interest but allows you to convert it into one common share at a set price of $20. If the price of the common share goes up to $30, you may decide to convert your bond into a common share, thereby giving up your 5% interest but gaining $10 or 50% in share value. These typically pay a slightly lower rate of interest than a bond because there is the potential benefit of a greater return by converting it into shares.

Mutual Funds (High): These are probably one of the best known investment products on the market due to the millions of dollars that are spent advertising and marketing them. There are literally thousands of mutual funds in Canada alone. And even with this number of funds and the millions of advertising dollars, they tend to be the product most misunderstood by investors. A mutual fund is a trust that has a manager who purchases a number of stocks and/or bonds and/or other investment products, such as commodities, in the hope of generating substantial returns. When you purchase a mutual fund, you are issued units in that fund that represent a proportionate ownership of all the stocks, bonds, and investment products held within the fund. As those investments go up or down, so does the value of your investment in the fund. One of the greatest benefits of this type of investment is your ability to take a small amount of money and invest it in a diverse group of investments. You also get to have your money managed by a professional money manager, who you would not be able to access on your own because you may not have enough investment assets. Typically, you can buy and sell your mutual funds on most business days. The type of fund you are investing in will determine the overall risk level, but I've classified these as high risk because the majority of funds tend to invest in high-risk investments. One of the downfalls of mutual funds is the cost associated with them. This cost is about two to three times higher than simply purchasing the same investments yourself. As well, most mutual funds tend not to outperform their equivalent index and, therefore, you may be better off simply purchasing the index itself.

Index Units (High): These are units or shares that represent a specified index. These indexes are typically stock exchanges or sub-indexes of those stock exchanges. For example, you could buy the Toronto Stock Exchange index, which represents the 300 largest companies that trade on the Toronto Stock Exchange. If the stock exchange goes up, then your investment in the index goes up, and vice versa. Alternatively, you could buy index units in a sub-index of the Toronto Stock Exchange. For example, you could invest in the financial services index, which holds all the major banks and insurance companies, so if those stocks go up, then your index units go up.

Index units typically trade on the stock exchange and the fees associated with them are 75 to 90% less than most mutual funds. As most index units are associated with high-risk investments, they themselves become high risk.

Exchange Traded Funds (ETFs) (High): These are very much like mutual funds. They can invest in a variety of investments within the fund, like a mutual fund, but they trade on a stock exchange, like an index fund or stock. The advantage of ETFs is that they tend to be less expensive than mutual funds because there is less involved in their administration and management So, with ETFs, you can get professional money management that may outperform the indexes, while keeping the cost 30 to 50% lower than mutual funds. The difference between ETFs and index units is that the ETF can be invested in just about any listed security, while index units must invest in those securities that make up the index.

Other non-traditional investment products, such as segregated funds, hedge funds, real estate investment trusts, life insurance, options, futures, commodities, and physical assets like real estate, rental property, precious metals and gems, collectibles, and art can also be investment options. Most of these are more complex, very high risk products. You should seek the assistance of investment professional that specializes in these types of investments before considering them.

Understanding Investment Risk

The basic theory of investment risk and the explanation of risk vs. return comes from human nature. The theory goes that if you have a choice to take more risk or less risk to achieve the same outcome, you will choose less risk every time. Therefore, in order to achieve a greater result or return, you will need to take more risk.

Putting Risk into Perspective

One of the easiest ways to reduce investment risk is to understand what return you need to achieve. Many financial advisors skip this step and tell you that they will get big returns and everything will be fine. The problem with this is that it is your money with which they are taking unnecessary risk.

Let's look at an example to explain this point. If you have $100,000 saved for retirement in 15 years and you plan to contribute $400 a month to end up with $500,000 at retirement, what return do you need to achieve? In this scenario, you would need to achieve about an 8.5% annual rate of return. So, if your advisor is always trying to achieve a 12 to 15% return, thereby risking that you could take a 20 to 30% loss, they are taking more risk than you need and jeopardizing your chance of reaching your goal.

If you feel that to achieve your goal you have to take more risk than you are prepared to take, then you may need either to increase your input or decrease the amount you need to achieve. Either of these choices will reduce the amount of return required and, therefore, the amount of risk that needs to be taken.

Other Forms of Investment Risk

If you think that buying GICs or Canada Savings Bonds is risk-free—you're wrong! Aside from volatility risk, investments face numerous other risks, depending on what you invest in. Here are a few of the most common risks to be aware of:

Interest Rate Risk: This typically affects the value of bonds much more than stocks. As explained earlier, if interest rates rise in value, the new bonds that are coming out will be more valuable than the existing bonds, which have lower interest rates. Therefore, those existing bonds will need to be reduced in price to become more attractive to buyers.

Political Risk: This is the risk that an investment's returns could decline due to political changes or instability in the country's government, foreign policies, or actions. An example may be that an oil company goes into a country and spends a lot of money building the necessary infrastructure to extract oil, but then the government changes its policy and simply takes over everything that has been done and kicks the company out of the country.

Inflation Risk: This is where the buying power of your money is eroded by inflation. So if you earn a 4% rate of return, but inflation is at 5%, you are actually losing money every year in terms of buying power.

Currency Risk: This is the risk of loss caused by change in the value of foreign exchange. For example, if you used Canadian dollars in 2005 when they were trading at 70 cents US to purchase a US$100 stock (CDN$142) and over the last seven years that stock has gone up 30%, then the stock is now worth US$130. But because the Canadian dollar has risen to par with the U.S. dollar, you have actually lost CDN$12 over the same time.

Credit Risk: This is usually associated with the bond market. When the credit rating or credit worthiness of the bond is downgraded, the price of the bond usually falls, and vice versa.

Liquidity Risk: This can affect all investment products. It is the risk that you will be unable to sell your investment and, therefore, have to reduce its value in order to entice buyers. This can often happen with stocks that have very low trading volumes and other investments that don't have a secondary market, like a stock exchange, for them to be sold on. Investments such as private placements and partnerships are good examples.

Now that we have a better perspective on risk, we'll start to look at how to invest and some best practices.

The "Stop Losing Big" Principle

This very simple concept seems to be one of the hardest to follow. The rule goes that if you never lose more than 10%, you never need to achieve big returns to get back to where you were. To use a very simple example:

if you have $100 and you lose 10%, you have $90. To get $90 back up to
$100, you only need to achieve an 11% rate of return. If you have $100
and you lose 50%, you have $50. To get $50 back up to $100, you need a
100% return.

This principle can be taken one step further to be applied against
your overall assets. In the illustration we have three bowls that hold
personal assets.

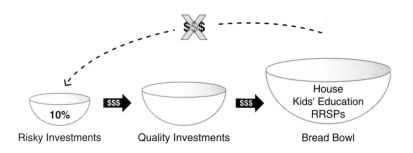

if you have $100 and you lose 10%, you have $90. To get $90 back up to
$100, you only need to achieve an 11% rate of return. If you have $100

The objective of this game is to get your bread bowl to be as large as possible. Your bread bowl is the bowl that holds all the assets that you never
want to risk losing. For many people, it would include things such as their
house, their retirement savings, their children's education, and maybe their
spouse's money—those assets you just do not want to touch or risk substantial loss to.

The medium-sized bowl is where you may have a number of your
investments and high-quality assets, yet these may be assets you're willing
to take greater risk with.

The smallest bowl is left for your risky investments, assets, or activities. Maybe you or your spouse feels that you could be the best investment
manager out there. You could take no more than 10% of your assets, put
them into a discount brokerage account, and see if you could outperform
the investment professionals. If you do phenomenally well and pick the
next Apple stock, you can transition some of the profits from this success
into your other two bowls. If you lose all the money, all you have lost is
about 10%. To recover from this you would only need to achieve an 11%
rate of return on the rest of your assets. This bowl could also be used

for substantial discretionary spending and other risky activities, such as gambling or expensive hobbies.

> Hard Rule: Money only moves from the smaller bowls into the bigger bowls. You can never replenish the small, risky bowl with assets from the larger bowls. You can only replenish the smaller bowl using a maximum of 10% of existing income.

Asset Allocation

Studies have proven time and again that more than 80% of a portfolio's return over time is based on how it is allocated among the various asset classes. Once the optimal asset allocation is determined, it then needs to be reviewed in the context of taxation and sheltering.

All too often I see portfolios where there are tax-efficient investments inside a tax-sheltered account and inefficient tax investments in a non-tax-sheltered account. This is generally caused by each account having its own asset allocation rather than all the accounts being looked at as one big account and the asset allocation being determined from there. Viewing all accounts as one big account can help to ensure that all the least tax-efficient income (interest) is sheltered in registered accounts (RRSP, TFSA), and the most tax-efficient income (dividends) is held in the non-registered accounts. This strategy also helps to reduce the number of trades that need to be made, as you will be able to hold the entire position of one investment in one account rather than several small positions in many accounts.

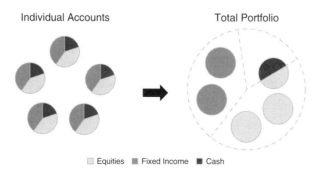

Individual Accounts　　　Total Portfolio

▢ Equities　▨ Fixed Income　■ Cash

Diversification

You always hear advisors and the media talking about diversifying your portfolio, and they all seem to have a different opinion on how you should do it! It can be by industry, asset class, nationality, currency, or product. Although no one can say which is best, the fundamental concept of diversification is sound.

My rules for diversification are:

Never invest more than 5% in any one thing. This way, if that investment turns sour and you lose everything (worst case scenario), you won't be too badly hurt.

Never invest more than 20% in any one industry or sector. This helps to avoid a major loss if one sector takes a large hit due to uncontrollable or unforeseeable events. (An example might be the oil and gas sector if oil prices were to collapse.)

Never focus on just one asset class. Just owning stocks or just owning bonds can result in significant fluctuations in your assets due to the mood or volatility of the sector.

Don't forget about other asset classes: Real estate is the largest asset class for many people, but owning too much could be detrimental to your finances, especially given that most real estate is heavily leveraged (mortgaged), so a small change in price can have a big impact on your net worth.

Your company: Some people think they need never diversify from the company they work for. In some cases, people have more than 90% of their net worth tied to their employer. They work for a big bank or utility company, and they have their pension there, they participate in an employee stock purchase plan, they are awarded shares and options as bonuses, and before they know it, they are way overextended in one investment. If the company were to go under, these people would lose not only their income, but their pensions, stocks, and options also would become worthless, and they would end up in serious financial trouble. Many individuals in this situation never think about the risk because they tend to work for the biggest and best companies. They simply don't believe their company will fail. Here is a list of a few of the biggest and best of recent years who are no longer with us:

- Enron: Once the largest energy supplier in North America
- Nortel: World-leading telecommunications provider
- Tyco: A multinational, multibillion-dollar conglomerate
- WorldCom: One of the largest telecommunications companies
- Lehman Brothers: A bank that had been around for more than 100 years

And if it wasn't for the government bailouts, companies such as General Motors, Air Canada, AIG Insurance, and others would have gone bankrupt as well. Just because you work for a very large, profitable company now does not mean that it will always be large and profitable. It is far better to diversify into other assets than to lose absolutely everything.

When to Buy and When to Sell

There's a saying that goes along the lines of: "The easiest thing to do is to buy a stock; the hardest thing to do is to sell it." I think the reason why it is easy to buy a stock is because we get excited about something and just go ahead and do it. I think that's part of human nature. What ends up happening when we become emotionally involved in the decisions we make is that we believe we are smarter than we are. And because we never like to admit when we're wrong, selling a stock becomes a hard thing to do. The disgrace of failure if the stock has gone down, or the temptation of greed if the stock has gone up, prevents us from making the decision to sell. Here are some fundamental rules to use when buying and selling stocks:

When buying an investment: Before purchasing any investment, you need to do your homework. This starts with looking at your overall financial situation, understanding your current situation, and assessing how each investment will fit in and help you achieve your goals. Once you determine that the investment makes sense in relation to the rest of your finances and the goals you're trying to achieve, you can move on to the next step.

Stop listening to the noise: Too many times, people get caught up in the hype and propaganda associated with an investment and don't take a close enough look to see whether or not it makes sense for them. The best thing you can do is to turn off the television; stop reading newspapers, magazines, and blogs; and take a look at the fundamentals of the investment you're considering purchasing. Look at leading indicators to see whether or not the predicted future growth of the investment is warranted and go out and get an education in both micro- and macroeconomics. Many times, investments have had very attractive balance sheets and exciting products, yet the stock has done very poorly due to economic circumstances and other factors.

Have a plan to sell your investment before purchasing it: Putting a systematic plan in place to sell the investment prior to owning it will help ensure you have a solid strategy to get in and out.

Don't catch a falling knife: One lesson we've all been taught (or learned the hard way) is that if a knife is falling, get out of the way. If you try to catch a falling knife, you will likely end up being badly cut. The same is true with a stock that is falling quickly and substantially. A classic example would be Nortel during its fall from grace, when in a short time the shares fell from $125 to $80. Many investors felt that this was a great opportunity to buy the stock at a cheap price, only to watch the stock continue to fall and fall and fall until Nortel went bankrupt.

Never sell at the top; never buy at the bottom: It is impossible for anybody to truly be able to define the specific point in time that a stock has reached its peak or its bottom.

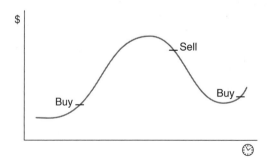

As you can see in the illustration, you want to buy the stock after it has bottomed out and has started to go higher. The reason for this is that you never know whether the stock is going to keep going down. My opinion is that it is better to pay a little bit more for a stock knowing it's going higher than to buy a stock not knowing which direction it's going in. The same is true when you sell a stock: you just never know if it's going to continue to go higher and higher. So it's better to wait for the stock to show that it's going to start declining and take slightly less profit than to just sell a stock and watch it continue to rise further and further, missing out on substantial gains.

One Frank Thought:

A favourite saying of mine is, "No one has ever lost money taking a profit!" This is to say that if you do end up selling your investments at a profit and they do continue to go up, you can't beat yourself up for it. You've taken a profit, made money, and that's the important thing.

Take emotion out of investing: Too many people allow their egos and emotions to interfere with their overall investments. Although easier said than done, it is important to understand that if an investment is going well, it may not continue to do so, and if an investment is not going well, it may well do worse. Understanding that there are other investments that have an opportunity to appreciate more than the one you're in can help you to make the decision to sell at the appropriate time.

Where to Invest Your Money Based on the Value of Assets to Be Invested

As you will see, the tools on the website include a recommendation about which investment products are the most suitable for the level of investable assets you have. These recommendations take into consideration the frequency of investing, the costs associated with individual purchases of investments, the costs associated with the investments themselves, and the risk-return opportunity for each one. In Chapter 12 I will discuss which types of investment advisors may be appropriate given the amount of investable assets you have.

> **$0–$60,000:** At this stage of investing, you are just starting out. This can be a very confusing time because all these concepts and ideas seem new to you. Often you're getting people from all over giving you their thoughts and opinions about what's best. You need to keep in mind that what they are giving you is their opinion, based on their experiences and on the investments and assets that they have. In order for you to prosper and grow your investment assets from this level, you need to seriously consider the time frame in which you're going to be using your money. Your goal should be a minimum of five years, and possibly up to 45 years. Given these factors, mutual funds may be your best option. Although not the least expensive of the investment options, mutual funds do allow you to access professional money managers, significantly diversify your investments through a single product, and provide an easy way to make small purchases on a regular basis.

> **$60,000–$200,000:** Now that you're getting the hang of investing and starting to build and grow your wealth, it is time to move more and more of your assets toward competitive products that are less expensive. At this stage you still need broad diversification but generally at a lower cost. This is where ETFs and index units really start to make a lot of sense. When it comes to ETFs, you still get professional money management and broad diversification but usually at half the cost of mutual funds. With index units you get an even more cost-effective product, just without professional money management.

> **$200,000–$500,000:** At this stage you're starting to get into the realm of a high net worth or wealthy client. You can start creating your own index fund or your own mutual fund by purchasing individual stocks and bonds. This ultimately ends up giving you greater flexibility and more options for diversification and can be done at substantially cheaper costs than buying mutual funds, ETFs, or index units. You do

give up having a professional money manager, but with assets at this level, you may attract other professional money managers and investment advisors.

$500,000–$1 Million: At this level of investable assets, in conjunction with individual stocks and bonds, you may start adding additional investment products, such as preferred shares, convertible debentures, and private placements. You may also look at more sophisticated investment products and solutions, such as additional real estate, life insurance, and derivative products. The goal here is to start moving away from growth and toward asset preservation and income generation.

$1 Million Plus: At this level you're making investments similar to the ones you were making at the previous level, but you're starting to add even more sophisticated assets, such as partnerships and hedge funds, while implementing more sophisticated asset-preservation and tax-reduction strategies and considering institutional-style money management. With assets at this level, it becomes worthwhile to pay some additional fees to bring in expertise to help you manage these areas.

The Best Investment: *Knowledge!* For many of us, this will come in the form of reading books like this one or maybe taking a night or correspondence course. Although learning about personal finance is not everyone's cup of tea, everyone can at least have a proper, comprehensive financial plan prepared. This can be an educational experience itself and pay dividends in the form of reducing your investment risk, increasing your income, saving you thousands of dollars in taxes, and, most of all, providing peace of mind through a better quality of life.

So, looking back at the investments section, you want to make sure you have a solid understanding of where you are and what you're using your money for. Knowing what you need to achieve with your investments and, from that, determining what level of risk needs to be accounted for helps put risk in perspective. By following some fundamental rules of investment management, you can reduce the myriad risks that could jeopardize your overall goals, plans, and lifestyle. One of the biggest considerations is your knowledge level and emotional attachment to your investments.

One Frank Thought

Investing is not for everyone. Many people have absolutely no desire to deal with and manage investments on their own. One of the most dangerous things you can do is to hire an investment advisor to manage your money and completely ignore the investments yourself. Even if you don't like dealing with them, you still have to, because as the saying goes, "No one cares more about your money than you do." Too many times I have met people who come to me with their portfolios, complaining about how horribly their investments have performed for years on end and how little advice — or no advice — has come from their investment advisor. No matter who you hire to help you manage your investments, it is still your responsibility to monitor those investments, ask questions of your advisor, and challenge the answers given to you.

Janice

In her late twenties, Janice was a woman with a serious plan. She was determined to retire as soon as possible, preferably within the next 10 years. She had been studying with some of the popular financial gurus and had decided that she was going to create enough passive income streams (that is, income she didn't have to work for) to reach financial freedom at a young age. To that end she had joined a large network marketing company, quickly building her customer base to the point where she could leave her job as an administrative assistant. Thanks to her advancement bonuses, she was earning several thousand dollars per month and working at the business full time. Then her father passed away suddenly, and she was left with an inheritance of close to $300,000.

Grieving, but excited about how this would accelerate her plans, she began looking for suitable investments. She looked at real estate and day trading, but keeping in mind that her goal was passive income, she connected with a financial advisor who specialized in limited partnerships and private placements. He assured her that, while there was some risk in investing her money this way, his research was very thorough and that he had a great track record. Janice didn't think to ask for references, she just wanted to get going.

After looking at several businesses, Janice chose to become a limited partner in a new auto repair shop. For $150,000 she was able to purchase 15% ownership in the company. She was thrilled that she would be receiving regular profit dividends and that, as the company grew, her investment would grow with it.

Janice continued her work with the network marketing company and put the rest of her inheritance into a series of short-term bonds while she waited for her next investment opportunity to arise. She received her first quarterly update right on time, saying that the shop was about to open and that everything was going according to plan. Three months after that she didn't hear anything, and when she called her advisor to find out how it was going at the shop, she felt he was being evasive. She asked him what was happening, and he admitted he wasn't sure: the shop owner hadn't been returning his calls. With a sinking feeling, Janice drove by the shop and saw the "For Lease" sign in the window.

Long story short, the business owner was in the process of negotiating bankruptcy protection and, six months after that, her money was gone. That was when Janice came to me.

Janice realized that she needed advice she could trust. As I had been her parents' advisor for many years, her mother recommended she meet with me. Janice had gained a valuable education, and she obviously wasn't going back to the first advisor. He specialized in risky private ventures because he was not legally allowed to help people invest in regulated vehicles like stocks and mutual funds.

She arrived at our first meeting with her goals, balance statement, and budget prepared and packaged in a binder. But I could tell that she was still ashamed of her recent error.

I tried to ease her pain a bit by pointing out that she had just learned an incredibly valuable financial lesson and that, at her age, she could recover from the loss. It had taught her caution, and the good news was that she still had half of her inheritance to invest in a different way. Plus, with her increasing income, wisdom would be more valuable than the money she had lost.

We were able to develop a financial plan that diversifies her investments over several growth-oriented assets while she continues her education toward becoming a sophisticated investor. The next time an opportunity presents itself, Janice will be ready to do her due diligence. In the meantime, she has a diversified portfolio of ETFs and index units, with 10% of her capital in a brokerage account that she uses to make stock plays.

Remaining mindful of her desire to generate passive income streams, she has also taken 20% of her capital to invest in real estate as a second-mortgage holder through a local broker in Hamilton. While Janice and I don't always see eye-to-eye on her investment choices, she has listened to me and now has the majority of her capital in lower-risk vehicles that provide great returns and are moving her toward financial freedom while she continues to build her network marketing business.

Alex and Juliette

When Alex and Juliette came to see me six years ago, Alex was changing something in his accounts almost every day. This wasn't surprising as he had 17 mutual funds at four different banking institutions and a discount brokerage trading account that he self-managed.

When I asked Alex why he had so many different accounts, he replied that he had wanted to ensure he was diversified, and that over the years he had simply added new accounts when he learned something new about investing. His portfolio was a record of every investment trend to sweep through Canada in the last 25 years. I was relieved to see that less than 10% of his capital was in the brokerage account.

I explained that buying lots of different funds did not necessarily mean he was diversified, and to illustrate this we examined three of his biggest funds—from three different banks. Alex's funds were heavily weighted toward Canadian equities, which meant that, although he had three different funds from three different companies, he was invested in almost exactly the same "blue-chip" Canadian companies in each. In fact, of all the companies held in the funds, more than 10% of the shares were from one company, and three companies made up 15% of the investment. This was hardly the security in diversity he had been looking for.

Juliette, on the other hand, perhaps to counterbalance her husband's tendency to invest in too many assets, had her savings in a savings account. All of her savings. Making less than 2% interest per year. When I asked her why, she explained that she had wanted her money to be safe. I explained to her that in a traditional savings account, she was actually losing money each year due to inflation and service fees. She agreed to move her money to a high-interest savings account while we developed their financial plan.

Once they had completed their goals and balance sheet it was obvious that Alex's portfolio was too heavily weighted toward growth. They were both hoping to retire by the time they turned 65 and, with a time horizon of less than 10 years, it was important to decrease their investment risk. Looking at their long-range goals for a secure retirement and the ability to start education funds for their future grandchildren, we were able to properly set up portfolios for both of them.

I understood Juliette's desire to create a conservative portfolio in line with her risk tolerance, and so we developed a strategy involving a high-interest savings account, market-linked GICs that would guarantee her principal, and highly rated corporate bonds that had a higher interest rate than government bonds. That was as much risk as she was willing to tolerate with her own money.

Alex's portfolio was a bit more of a challenge. We rearranged his investments to ensure that interest-paying vehicles were in tax-sheltered RRSP accounts, while his extra capital was used to purchase dividend-paying stocks. We moved his sizeable portfolio away from its emphasis on balanced funds and common shares to a much stronger preferred-shares position to reduce volatility risk. We also invested a significant percentage in bonds and market-linked GICs to provide income and more security. I confess that he was quite resistant to my conservative suggestions, but the approach was validated in 2008 when the market began its slide. Although their portfolio took a hit, the total loss was only around 7%, not the 20 to 30% that they would have lost had they been invested purely in stocks.

We reviewed their life insurance and changed the beneficiary to pay out to each other and their daughter to avoid the proceeds being subject to probate through their estate and modified their wills so that money would be directed toward the education of any grandchildren who might need it at the time of their passing. Finally, they purchased long-term care insurance to ensure that if they needed care, they would not be a financial burden on their daughter or each other. They have reported that the stress about their finances has been pretty much eliminated and that their relationship has improved now that they aren't second-guessing each other's decisions.

Chapter Summary

- Be aware of and learn about the various investment options that are available.
- Recognize that you do not need to participate in all the various types of investment assets.
- Take all the forms of risk and put them into context by determining whether they are risks that affect you or risks that you need to take.
- Set up your investment assets so that you are continually growing your net worth through high-quality, risk-appropriate investments.
- Identify the proper asset allocation for the types of returns you're looking to achieve.
- Properly diversify your investments, as well as your income and pensions.
- Never try to sell at the top or buy at the bottom.
- Identify which types of investment products are most appropriate given your level of investable assets.

How To Eat An Elephant.ca—Web Tools

Investment Allocation Calculator

This calculator is designed to help you determine how to allocate your investments among the most common asset classes (cash, fixed income, equities). You can use it to help you to plan your investment portfolio. The report will show you what percentage of your investments should be invested in each category and give you an approximate annual rate of return, both before and after tax.

> **STEP ONE**: Log into www.howtoeatanelephant.ca and select the **Investment Allocation Calculator** from the menu page.
>
> **STEP TWO**: Enter the name of the portfolio, the value to be invested, the year that you will need these funds, the percentage of the funds that you will need at that point, and click on the **Add** button. With some goals you will not need all the money the very first day. For example, if you are building your dream house, you may need $400,000, but you may only need $150,000 of that on day one.
>
> **STEP THREE**: Once you have entered this information for all portfolios and you wish to determine the investment allocation, click on the **Save** button followed by the **Get Report** button.
>
> **STEP FOUR**: Here you are presented with your report, which you can download and print as a PDF document.

This report is designed to help you determine how to diversify your portfolio among the general asset classes and to determine what may be a reasonable rate of return. It will show you how much tax you may pay for a non-registered investment account. It is not intended to replace professional advice. Use it during consultations with an investment advisor who can help you to choose the appropriate investment products to accomplish your goals.

Now let's see the types of investment to invest in and who you should work with to help you invest your money.

How To Eat An Elephant.ca—Web Tools

Investment Based on Assets Tool

This tool is designed to help you understand the types of assets in which you may consider investing, where you may wish to have your money managed, and gives you a rough idea of how much you should expect to pay in management fees.

> **STEP ONE:** Log into www.howtoeatanelephant.ca and select the **Investment Based on Assets Tool** from the menu page.
>
> **STEP TWO:** Here you are presented with your report, which you can download and print as a PDF document.
>
> **STEP THREE:** Verify the list of investment assets that has been pre-populated from your **Net Worth Tool**. If there is anything missing or incorrect, please go back to it and make the appropriate changes.

This report can be very helpful in choosing the types of advisors to interview. It will provide you with knowledge of the investments they should be recommending and an approximate range of management fees you may expect to pay. This report is not meant to replace professional advice.

10

TAX PLANNING

*Taxes, after all, are dues that we pay for the privileges of member-
ship in an organized society.*

—*Franklin D. Roosevelt*

WHEN PEOPLE ASK ME WHAT financial planning is, I explain that most of
it is really about the management of our tax system and processes. When
preparing a financial plan, the majority of my time is spent dealing with
tax-planning tools, such as RRSPs, tax-free savings accounts, dividend tax
credits, capital gains exemptions, trusts and corporations, life insurance,
tax shelters, and so on. These are all tools that are used to manage and
minimize taxation.

Principle of taxation: the government always gets paid!

Once you accept this principle and keep it in the back of your mind
while thinking about financial- and tax-planning strategies, most of these
strategies will begin to make much more sense. Tax-planning strategies are
used to reduce the tax payable in high-income years by deferring them to
low-income years or from a high-income taxpayer to a low-income taxpayer.
If you believe there's a way to legally avoid paying tax, you are wrong.

The government has general anti-avoidance rules (GAAR), which allow it to claim the taxation and penalize you for avoiding paying it in the first place. However, there is good news: the government has put in place a series of tax-management tools to help individuals decide when to pay their taxes and how much to pay (with many restrictions). The first trick is to know that these tools exist; the second is to know how to use and apply them!

As we go through this chapter, I will help you learn about some of these tools and understand the different deductions and credits. This should change the way you think about taxes and help you to better understand basic tax-saving principles.

One Frank Thought

I'm always frustrated that everybody believes they pay half their income in taxes. The reality is the majority of Canadians pay less than 30% of their income in the form of income tax.

How Much Income Tax Do We Pay?

When you look at your paycheque, it may appear as if a large portion of your pay is going to tax. The reality is that you are likely paying 30% or less in the form of income tax. Other deductions, such as CPP and EI premiums, are deducted from your pay and magnify the perception that you're paying a higher income tax rate. What we fail to remember is that the contributions to CPP provide us with a pension down the road. So, in a sense, those contributions are forced savings, providing an income for us during retirement.

There are many other deductions that also come off our paycheques, including money toward health insurance, disability insurance, union or professional dues, pension or RRSP contributions, gym memberships, and maybe other taxable benefits. When you add all of these together, it creates the perception that half of your income is going toward taxes, but in reality a large portion of the deductions are going toward savings and insurance to provide you with greater security.

Understanding the Difference between Average Tax Rate and Marginal Tax Rate

Your average tax rate is pretty straightforward. You take the total amount of tax you paid and divide it by your total income. For example, if you earned $75,000 in Alberta, you would pay $17,659 in taxes (2012). This works out to an average tax rate of 23.54%.

Your marginal tax rate is slightly more complicated. In Canada, we have a progressive taxation system. This means that the more money you earn, the more tax you pay, i.e., your taxes get progressively higher. The government has constructed a series of tax brackets that tax you at a higher rate as your income goes up. Once you earn more money in a higher tax bracket, the money earned in that higher bracket gets taxed at that higher rate. That higher rate then becomes your marginal tax rate.

Marginal rates of tax vary widely from province to province but are approximately (2012):

- 24% on income from $10,822 to $42,707
- 36% on income from $42,708 to $85,414
- 42% on income from $85,415 to $132,406
- 46% on income over $132,406

Tax Deduction vs. Tax Credit: Which Is Better?

A deduction, or a "write off," reduces your taxable income—the income on which the total amount of tax is calculated. So if you earn $75,000 in Alberta and have a $1,000 write off, you will have to pay tax on only $74,000. The difference in tax savings is only $320, so it is still costing you $680 to purchase that item. (RRSPs are an example of a tax deduction.)

One Frank Thought

I routinely hear people comment that they're buying something because they can write it off, or that buying it is no big deal as it is a write off. What they're failing to realize is that for each $100 they spend, the item is still costing them between $54 and $76 of their own money. Therefore, it is still a good idea to assess the value of the item or service that you are purchasing and negotiate the best price possible, rather than just going ahead and buying it and saying, "Oh, I can write this off!" The bottom line is that it is still money out of your pocket, just a little bit less of it.

A tax credit is a direct reduction in tax. This means that for every $100 of tax credits, you reduce your tax payable by $100. For example, if you had to pay $1,000 in taxes and you had $100 in tax credits, you would only have to pay $900. (A political party contribution or charitable contribution is considered to be a tax credit.)

Refundable Tax Credits vs. Non-Refundable Tax Credits

Refundable credits are always worth what they say they are worth. Taxes withheld from your paycheque or taxes paid through instalments are refundable credits. Non-refundable credits become worthless once you reach the point of paying no tax at all for the year. An example of a non-refundable tax credit is the basic personal exemption. The basic personal exemption is a tax credit of more than $10,800 a year that every person is entitled to. This gets multiplied by the lowest tax bracket (15%) so you get a tax credit (reduction in your taxes) of a little more than $1,600.

There are several tax deductions and credits that you can claim, and I strongly encourage you to use tax software or a tax professional to help you determine which ones you qualify for. Some examples of these include credits for:

- Spouses or dependent children
- Child care expenses
- Children's fitness activities
- Tuition fees
- Education
- Textbooks
- Scholarships or bursaries
- Interest on student loans

- Costs associated with disabilities
- Child and spousal support payments
- Medical expenses
- Political contributions
- Charitable contributions
- Public transit passes
- A first-time home purchase
- Legal fees associated with obtaining income

Let's take a look at some of the more common tax-planning strategies and solutions that are available today.

Registered Retirement Savings Plans (RRSPs)

As you read in Chapter 8, these programs can be used to defer paying taxes on income until a later date, when you will likely have less income and, therefore, pay tax at a lower rate when you withdraw from the RRSP than you would have at the time that you contributed to it.

Think of RRSPs as a tax-deferral tool and not a retirement savings plan. If you end up with a year where your income has dropped substantially— whether due to being laid off or fired from your job, leave of absence, maternity leave, or leave to provide medical care or attendant care—you may seriously consider withdrawing funds from your RRSP to help support you during this lower-income time. You should be aware that this may jeopardize your financial security and plans for retirement, so it is best to do it with help and advice from a certified financial planner.

If you are in the high-income tax bracket, an RRSP contribution can provide a large tax deduction and help to save you thousands of dollars in taxes during this high-income year. If it's been an expensive year and you haven't been able to save sufficient funds, or as much as you would like, for your RRSP contribution, you can consider using other existing assets and contributing them in-kind. For example, you may have some GICs at the bank worth $10,000: you can simply transfer these GICs into an RRSP and receive a tax contribution receipt. Maybe you have some shares or stocks in a company or maybe some mutual funds that are in a non-registered investment savings account. You could transfer those into an RRSP at fair market value and receive a full RRSP contribution tax deduction. However, this can create a tax liability itself, as the Canada Revenue Agency (CRA) considers the investment to have been sold when it is transferred into the RRSP (i.e., you will have a deemed disposition). For example, you could own some shares in a company that you originally purchased for $1,000 and that now have a value of $5,000. When you transfer those shares into your RRSP at the fair market value of $5,000, you will receive an RRSP tax contribution receipt of $5,000, but you will also create a $4,000 capital gain, half of which you will need to claim as taxable income. If you're planning to use this strategy, it is best to wait until January or February of the following year to make the contribution so that you receive the tax contribution of $5,000 against the previous year's taxable income but do not have to claim the capital gain until the following tax year.

One Frank Thought

Be careful not to contribute assets in-kind that have a capital loss. Although you will still have a deemed disposition on the fair market value of assets transferred into your RRSP, CRA will not allow you to use the capital loss against your capital gains.

Another way to minimize your taxes is to pay the fees for administration, trustees, investment management, and counselling related to your RRSPs from the funds of your RRSP. Management fees that are paid from RRSPs are not considered a withdrawal. They are simply fees paid for management of the assets. In a sense this makes them tax-deductible when they do not qualify as tax deductions. For example, let's say you had to pay $1,200 in fees for the management of your RRSP account. You could make a $1,200 contribution to your RRSP (provided you had room), receive a tax receipt, and then have the administrator withdraw the $1,200 to pay the fees. When the administrator withdraws the funds to pay the fees, there are no taxes due.

We will look at strategies and ways to withdraw money from RRSPs a little later in this chapter in the section on retirement tax planning.

The Home Buyers' Plan and Lifelong Learning Plan

These plans really provide no tax-planning benefits as they are simply loans from your RRSP. These plans allow you to withdraw money to help you purchase your first home or pay for recognized education from funds within your RRSP, rather than having to use other savings or borrow money. But you are required to repay these borrowed amounts according to a set schedule. If you fail to repay these funds to your RRSP, the designated amount to be repaid for that year becomes taxable income.

One Frank Thought

You may decide, if you have a very low income (in a year when you may not have the additional funds to make the repayment of the RRSP loan), to take the amount as taxable income in that year as you will be in a low tax bracket.

The government created these plans to help make it easier for Canadians to purchase their first home or further their education in the belief that this would help the country to prosper.

One Frank Thought

These programs are generally used by people who are younger, buying a house for the first time, and/or furthering their education. Younger people tend to have a lower income and, therefore, pay less tax. As these people grow and develop in their careers, they will end up in a higher tax bracket and can better use their money to contribute to RRSPs to get a tax deduction. I strongly encourage people to aggressively pay back these RRSP loans while they're in a lower-income tax bracket. Then, when they're in a higher-income tax bracket, the money available to contribute to RRSPs can be applied to reduce their taxable income and save them more tax dollars.

Income-Splitting

These are strategies to save taxes by shifting income from the hands of one family member in a high tax bracket to the hands of another family member in a lower tax bracket. As this obviously creates a substantial benefit to the individual and substantial liability to the government, CRA has done a very good job of removing or eliminating many income-splitting opportunities.

If CRA has not created a rule against your specific transaction, it can still apply its general anti-avoidance rules (GAAR) to the transaction. As I mentioned at the beginning of this chapter, the government always gets paid.

Pay all the expenses: A simple way to legally split income with a spouse is to have the high-income spouse pay all the bills and expenses, including the income taxes of the other spouse, so that all the income of the lower-income spouse can be put toward investments. The investment income would then be taxed in the hands of the lower-income spouse.

Employ spouse or child: Another strategy is to employ your spouse or children and pay them a salary that is considered to be reasonable for the services they perform. This benefit needs to be considered against the additional costs of payroll taxes, CPP contributions, and EI premiums. You may consider having your spouse provide these services on a contract basis rather than as an employee and allow them to take advantage of self-employment income, including writing off expenses.

Give your spouse a loan: When you loan assets to your spouse, any income that is derived from those assets is attributed back to you, unless you charge your spouse CRA's minimum prescribed rate of interest. Provided the assets can generate a return that is significantly higher than the prescribed rate of interest, this can work out substantially in your favour.

One Frank Thought

If you decide to go down the road of loaning your spouse money, be sure to properly document the loan and be able to clearly show payment of the interest on that loan, as well as income generated by the assets each and every year. Rather than simply having your spouse give you some cash as an interest payment while you're sitting on the couch watching TV, make a physical transfer from one account to another so that there is documented evidence of the payment made according to the loan agreement.

Fund your spouse's TFSA: You can contribute to your spouse's tax-free savings account up to his or her maximum allowable room. The investments are allowed to grow tax-free in your spouse's TFSA, thereby shifting assets from a high-income spouse to a low-income spouse.

Sell your assets to your spouse: When you sell your assets to your spouse at fair market value in exchange for consideration (equivalent assets, loan), any future income is taxed in the lower-income spouse's hands. Although this does create a tax liability to you as you have sold the assets, a transfer at fair market value may be beneficial where the assets are expected to produce a high return in the near future.

Investment Income

Understanding how various income and investment sources are taxed can help you to structure and plan where you want assets to be invested. Rearranging your existing investments so that you shelter the highest taxed investments can save you hundreds, sometimes thousands, of dollars.

There are essentially four types of investment income: interest income, dividend income, capital gains, and return of capital.

Interest income is taxed at the highest level. It is taxed the same way as employment income. Interest income is generated through savings accounts, GICs or bonds, debentures, and loans or mortgages. If you hold all of these investments in the tax shelter of an RRSP or TFSA, you can end up saving yourself thousands of dollars in taxes.

Dividend income can come in two forms: eligible dividends and ineligible dividends. Eligible dividends are any taxable dividend paid to a resident of Canada by a Canadian corporation that is designated by that corporation to be an eligible dividend. These dividends qualify the taxpayer for the dividend tax credit, which is used to reduce the amount of tax payable on all income. All other dividends are considered ineligible for the dividend tax credit. Suffice it to say that the majority of dividends paid to Canadians by Canadian corporations that trade on an exchange are eligible.

Eligible dividend income is the most tax-preferred income. Individuals could earn upward of $65,000 a year of eligible dividend income and not have to pay any taxes due to the dividend tax credit, provided they had no other income. Therefore, it makes a lot of sense to have dividend income-producing assets held outside registered accounts, such as RRSPs and tax-free savings accounts.

Capital gains: When you sell an asset for more than you paid for it, you have a capital gain. Only 50% of the value of the gain becomes taxable as income. For example, if you bought an investment at $1,000 and sold it for $2,000, you would have a $1,000 capital gain. Fifty percent of this $1,000 gain becomes taxable income. So you would have to add $500 to your overall income. Capital gains can be offset by capital losses on assets that are held outside of a registered account. So if you made that $1,000 gain on one investment and you lost $500 on another investment, you would only end up with a $500 capital gain, of which only 50% would be taxable income, i.e., you would only need to include $250 of the gain in your income.

Every individual is entitled to a lifetime capital gains exemption of up to $750,000 on certain small-business shares and farm and fishing properties. To understand if your business qualifies, be sure to speak with a tax professional.

Return of capital: Some trust structures, such as real estate investment trusts, income trusts, and some mutual funds pay monthly or quarterly distributions. A small portion of those distributions could be a return of the original capital that you invested. For example: Let's say you invested $1,000 into a resource fund that is paying a monthly distribution of $10. The resource fund is paying $5 in dividends and $5 in a return of your investment capital. At the end of two months, you will have received $10 in dividends and $10 of your original investments. So if you sell the investment at the end of the two months and get $1,000 for it, CRA will say you sold it for $1,000 but only paid $990 for it because you got back $10 of your original investment. This will result in a $10 capital gain, and you will have to pay tax on half of it.

Investing in Tax Shelters

Tax shelters are legally recognized investments that provide the investor with beneficial tax considerations. Most legal tax shelters are intentionally structured to encourage investment assets into an area that may otherwise have difficulty attracting them. Many common shelters include small-business corporations, scientific research, or exploration for oil, gas, metals, and minerals. Many times, these tax shelters carry much higher risks than other equivalent investments.

One Frank Thought

Investing in a tax shelter simply to reduce your tax liability in a given year, in exchange for taking significantly higher risk than you need to, may not make sense. To invest $1,000 to save $300 of taxes, only to lose $1,000, means you're $700 in the hole! We all hate to pay tax, but I think everyone can agree that this math doesn't make sense. Carefully consider investing in tax shelters to ensure that the investment matches with your goals and objectives.

Creating Tax-Deductible Interest

When you borrow money and invest it in assets that have an opportunity to generate income, you are allowed to write off the interest costs from that loan. One example of this might be getting a mortgage on a rental property and renting that property out. The interest on that mortgage becomes tax-deductible against the income that is generated from the rental. Another example may be that you borrow money from your spouse, pay him or her the minimum prescribed rate or higher rate of interest, and deduct that interest against the income generated by the assets you borrowed. Remember to document your interest payments.

Charitable Donations

Charitable donations entitle you to a tax credit. With the first $200, you will receive a tax credit worth about 24%, when provincial tax credits are taken into account. All donations above that level will give you a tax credit worth roughly 45%, with the provincial tax credit.

The maximum amount of donations you can claim in a year is 75% of your net income. If you have donated more than this in any given year, you can carry forward those donations and claim them in the following five years. In the year of death, donation amounts can be claimed up to 100% of your net income, and if there are still excess donations, your executor can go back to your previous tax year and claim them against up to 100% of that year's income.

There are many different ways to contribute to charitable organizations: donations of cash, gifts in-kind, cultural property, and ecologically sensitive land; gifts of life insurance; and using tools such as charitable remainder trusts and donor-advised funds. Each of these has its own advantages, disadvantages, rules, and restrictions. Below is some information on the most common forms of charitable donations. Be sure to speak with a certified financial planner to help you decide on the best way to donate money to a charity.

Cash donations: Probably one of the easiest ways to donate money to charity, but the least tax efficient. A $1,000 donation will give you about a $450 tax credit. The cost to you to make a $1,000 charitable donation is $550.

Gifts in-kind: There are many ways to donate in-kind to charities. One of the most common and effective ways of doing this is by donating publicly traded securities, employee stock options, shares, artwork, or real estate. When it comes to donating securities or employee stock options, it is done at fair market value. If the shares or stock options have appreciated and you have a capital gain, you do not have to pay tax on that capital gain. Let's look at an example of the difference between selling the shares and donating the cash vs. just donating the shares.

Let's say you paid $500 for shares that are now worth $1,000. If you sell the shares for $1,000 and donate the cash to a charity, you will have to claim $500 in capital gains and pay tax on $250. If your marginal tax rate is 40%, your tax bill will be $100. If you simply donate the shares worth $1,000, you will make the same charitable donation as if you donated cash, but now you won't have to pay the capital gains on those shares, thereby saving you $100 of taxes.

Certified cultural property and ecologically sensitive land: Donations of these types of property will be made at the property's fair market value, but again no taxable capital gain will arise. Interestingly enough, capital losses may be deductible in some circumstances.

Life insurance donations: With the use of permanent life insurance policies, such as whole life or universal life, you can transfer the ownership of the policy to the charity and have the charity become the beneficiary of the policy. The charity will issue you a tax receipt based on the cash surrender value of the policy, plus any accumulated dividends and interest. (If there are any policy loans, this amount will be subtracted from the tax receipt issued.) Should you continue to pay the premiums on the policy, each payment will be considered another charitable donation.

Another way to donate life insurance to a charity is to name the charity as the beneficiary of the life insurance policy. When you pass away, the value of the policy will then be donated to the charity, and the charitable donation tax receipt can be used to reduce your final income tax bill, as well as taxes from the previous year.

Charitable remainder trusts: In this situation, you wish the charity to be the capital beneficiary of your assets when you die, but while you are alive you still need those assets to generate income to support you. By setting up a charitable remainder trust, you transfer the assets into the trust, and during your lifetime, the trust pays any income to you; the capital will go to the charity on your death (otherwise known as the residual interest in the property). Charities like these because they get a vested right to the property immediately without having to worry about whether someone else will make a claim against those assets. These are good for the person making the donation as they get an immediate tax receipt based on the residual value at the time the trust is set up. They also still receive all the income generated from those assets for the rest of their life.

Donor-advised funds: These are another kind of special box. Remember we said that your RRSP and TFSA are special boxes where you can deposit cash or securities and have them managed and invested by a third party? Well, sometimes that third party is a for-profit financial institution, but it could be a charitable foundation. You, as an individual, have the ability to decide what is invested in the fund, and you can decide which charities will receive donations from this fund. Every calendar year the fund is required to donate a minimum of 3.5% of the value of the fund to recognized registered charities. While the funds are invested inside this box, they grow tax-free.

These funds allow you to maintain control of the asset by deciding how you want it to be invested and how much you donate to which charities. They are typically for people who are looking to make larger donations over an extended time. This traditionally was done through a charitable foundation, which required a lot more work to set up, run, and report. The costs were substantially higher than donor-advised funds as well.

To fully understand how charitable giving can influence your tax planning and reduce your lifetime tax bill, have a comprehensive financial plan prepared to better understand the impact of the various ways to make a difference in your community.

Retirement Tax Planning

It is very important to go into and be in retirement with a solid understanding of your financial situation. A survey carried out in January and February 2011 of Canadians between 55 and 70 years of age showed that 73% of those who had a comprehensive financial plan were confident and comfortable with their retirement situation.[*]

By preparing this plan, you can learn essential information:

- If you will outlive your money or not.
- How much of an estate you might leave.

---

[*] See: http://opinion.financialpost.com/2011/07/08/one-in-three-retirees-spending-more-than-they-expected/

- What your annual and lifetime tax bills will be.
- How much money you can draw from various income sources.
- How to structure your investments and income to reduce your annual tax bill.
- How to use different investment products and planning structures to reduce your tax bill every year.
- How to apply different planning ideas to reduce your final tax bill.

RRSPs Can Create a Large Tax Bill!

Many people have saved up and watched their RRSPs grow considerably to provide income for them in retirement. They have never paid tax on this money; it has been allowed to grow tax-free. When they start to withdraw the money, it must be included as taxable income. Upon death, the entire amount remaining in the RRSP must be included as part of the deceased's income in that year. Alternatively, it can be rolled over to a spouse or disabled dependent child and be part of their RRSP. If it can't be rolled over, then the entire amount becomes the income of the deceased and will likely be taxed at a very high rate.

For example, Jim, who is 67, dies suddenly from a heart attack and his RRSP worth $223,000 rolls over to his wife, Sarah, who is 70. Jim's RRSP assets are now part of Sarah's, giving her a total of $465,000. Sarah passes away three years later, and her now registered retirement income fund (RRIF) is worth $495,000. She designated her two sons to be equal beneficiaries of the fund. What Sarah didn't count on was that CRA will be the biggest beneficiary, as the entire amount of the RRIF will be considered her taxable income, and approximately 46% of it (i.e., $227,700) will have to be paid as tax!

Here are a few ways you can minimize the taxes on your RRSP:

- Start taking smaller amounts out of your RRSP earlier. This allows you to pay a smaller amount of tax (maybe 30%) over a series of years, rather than 46% in the final year.
- Shrink the RRSP by paying all fees for investment management and counsel from the RRSP. Depending on the size of your

investment portfolio, this could reduce your RRSP by 1.5% each and every year. This money, when withdrawn by the investment manager to pay fees, is not taxable.

When you are considering how much income to withdraw from your RRSP, be conscious of how much income you need and how your withdrawals might impact the amount of Old Age Security benefits you receive. In 2012, if your income was more than $69,562, then you would have seen your OAS benefit reduced at a rate of $0.15 for every dollar of taxable income over this amount.

To reduce the chances of this happening, there are a few things you can do:

- Withdraw more from your RRSP in years prior to turning 65. Your OAS benefits, starting at 65 (67 if you were born after March 1958), will be worth a maximum of $6,540 (2012). So if you retire at 60, consider withdrawing an extra $6,540 a year for the first five years to shrink your RRSP and reduce your future taxable income, while giving yourself a stable income all the way through retirement.
- Use non-registered investments and funds from your TFSA to supplement your income and reduce your taxable income to keep it below the OAS clawback threshold.
- Split your RRIF/RRSP income with your spouse. To do this, you have to be at least 65 and convert your RRSP to a RRIF. This will see your spouse (with less income) declare some of the RRIF as income and have it taxable in his or her hands, thereby reducing your taxable income below the OAS threshold.
- Split your pension income with your spouse. This is the same as splitting RRIF/RRSP income, but you can do it at any age (although most pensions do not allow withdrawals prior to age 55).
- Split your CPP credits with your spouse. As with splitting pensions and RRIF/ RRSP income, you can effectively split your CPP pension with your spouse. The difference here is that you both have to qualify for CPP. So if your spouse is younger than you

and has not qualified for CPP yet, or has never made a contribution to CPP, you will not be able to do this. Once your spouse qualifies for CPP, you can irrevocably elect to assign CPP credits to each other. So, in simple terms, if you have 10 CPP credits and your spouse has six, you have a combined total of 16 CPP credits. Therefore, each of you will be paid eight credits' worth of CPP. There can be a downside to doing this: if the person with fewer credits passes away early, the one who had more credits will be stuck with a smaller CPP income than they otherwise could have had.

- Base your RRIF withdrawals on the younger spouse's age. Basing the minimum RRIF withdrawal on a younger spouse's age reduces the minimum amount you have to withdraw from a RRIF, thereby giving you more control over how much to withdraw, which in turn gives you more control over your annual taxable income.

The Case for Using Spousal RRSPs

With a spousal RRSP, one spouse contributes money into an RRSP for the other spouse. The contributing spouse receives the tax credit, and his or her RRSP room is reduced. This used to be an effective way to split income in retirement by both spouses having nearly equal retirement savings.

With the changes made to retirement income-splitting rules a few years ago, spousal RRSPs became a less effective income-splitting tool in retirement. One situation where they can still be quite effective is when there is a plan to retire prior to the age of 65. If you have a relatively high income and your spouse has a relatively low income, and you plan to retire before the age of 65, you may seriously consider making contributions to a spousal RRSP so that you can split income in the first few years of retirement.

Because you are unable to split RRSP/RRIF income with your spouse before the age of 65, the use of spousal RRSPs—where you contribute assets into an account for your spouse—allows both of you to make smaller withdrawals from the two RRSP accounts, thereby reducing the overall tax bill.

One Frank Thought

Again, this is where preparing a comprehensive financial plan can help to give you the insight to make these decisions with confidence. How much you need to contribute to a spousal RRSP can be seen through one of these plans. You may not need to contribute a whole lot to a spousal RRSP because you may only need one, two, or maybe five years' worth of income-splitting. Once you reach the age of 65, you can convert your RRSP to a RRIF and start splitting the withdrawals with your spouse.

Additional Ways to Reduce Your Tax Bill

Once you have prepared your comprehensive financial plan, understood how much money (if any) you will have left as an estate, and planned to reduce your yearly and lifetime tax bills, use some of the following planning strategies and tools to more effectively reduce those tax bills:

Maximize the TFSAs: Once you have used up all the room in your TFSA, consider maxing out your children's TFSAs and possibly your grandchildren's as well (provided they are over 18). This can shelter non-registered assets for many years and reduce your personal tax bill each year. Understand that as soon as you deposit the money into their TFSAs, you no longer own the asset, and they are free to withdraw it at any time and do what they want with it. But if you can get them all to agree to leave it alone, you could shelter a lot of money in these plans.

For example, in 2012 the maximum limit on TFSA deposits could be as much as $20,000. If you have three married children, each with one child over the age of 18, you could potentially shelter up to $180,000 (three children, three children-in-law, three grandchildren × $20,000 each) and an additional $45,000 (9 × $5,000) each year after that!

Permanent Life Insurance: Another effective way to reduce your lifetime tax bill is to purchase a permanent life insurance policy. You take out a life insurance policy on yourself and pay $20,000 a year in premiums rather than investing that $20,000 in investments that pay dividends and interest that you have to pay tax on. This will create a guaranteed investment that will pay out tax- and probate-free to your heirs.

There are many other ways to increase your income in retirement while reducing your annual and lifetime tax bills. More advanced strategies, such as insurable annuities, reverse mortgages, family trusts, and personal corporations, are also available. It is important that you work with a tax- and financial-planning specialist to better understand which strategies make the most sense for your situation.

Without taking the entire financial picture into consideration, it is very difficult to find and decide which tax-planning strategies will be most effective. Working with a certified financial planner to prepare a comprehensive financial plan can help you to make better, more effective decisions that can save you thousands of dollars in taxes.

Jakub

Fifteen years ago, Jakub was flying high. He owned a successful renovation company that specialized in bathrooms and kitchens, and he and his wife had just purchased their dream home in Winnipeg's Tuxedo neighbourhood. When his wife presented him with divorce papers, he was angry, hurt, and completely shocked—he had thought everything was great. But his wife just couldn't take his long days and high stress. It didn't matter what home they lived in or how much money they had, she just didn't want to be in the marriage any longer. Jakub was shattered.

The divorce proceedings went smoothly. Jakub transferred half of his RRSP and other assets to his wife, though he retained sole ownership of his business in exchange for his half of the house. He also agreed to sizeable support payments for her and the kids. Unfortunately, over the next few years, his bitterness increased as he saw his ex living in his house, with his children, on his money, while he lived in an apartment by himself. Then, 10 years ago, the slow decline his business had been experiencing became a steep plummet, and it went under.

Things continued to fall apart for Jakub as he went from a successful contractor to an occasional labourer. He could no longer afford the high support payments required by his divorce agreement and, after draining his RRSP, was forced into personal bankruptcy. His wife had to sell their large home and move into a much smaller town-house with the children. Jakub's world became darker and darker, and he began drinking heavily. He eventually ended up on social assistance.

Then, as he emerged from bankruptcy three years ago, Jakub turned a corner. He began to attend a local church and meetings at Alcoholics Anonymous. He took a serious look at his life and saw the misery he was causing his ex-wife, his children, his family, and himself. He resolved to make a change and began by apologizing to his children, whom he had rarely seen while he was in the darkness of alcoholism, and to his ex, toward whom he had held so much bitterness.

He restarted his business, working with a government skills program to develop a business plan and get training in business finances so that he could keep a closer eye on the books. He actively promoted his business and was rewarded with rapid growth. He worked out careful budgets for his new company and for himself and focused on his list of short- and long-term goals.

Jakub also resolved to be smarter about his savings and investments and so he contacted me. Now in his late forties, he knows that he has to make the best use of the time available to ensure that he has enough money to retire and to create the life of his dreams. Starting from scratch has given him the opportunity to build his business and financial life in the best way possible. Starting with goals and budgets, we have developed a fairly aggressive financial plan to help maximize his returns while keeping in mind his desired retirement age. He is confident that his plan will guide him over the next 15 to 20 years.

While his income is still relatively low, he is focusing on investing in a TFSA, where the money will grow and be available tax-free, and on building up his RRSP contribution room to use when he is making much more money. As his income increases, he intends to use an RRSP to better control his taxable income and reduce his overall taxes.

He also plans to rebuild his relationship with his two children, now in their late teens, and is hopeful that they will welcome him back into their lives. His longer-term goals are now coming into play, and he intends to start building his estate and reducing his lifetime tax bill through a few different methods:

- He has taken out a life insurance policy on himself, with his children as beneficiaries, so that if something happens to him before his estate is firmly established, he will still leave behind a legacy.
- He has also designated a local addiction services charity as a one-third beneficiary on that life insurance policy.

Jakub has been through a lot of darkness, and now that he has fought his way back, he is feeling energized and determined to make a difference in his world, repair his relationships, and give back to the community that helped him when he was down.

Javier and Natalia

Natalia and Javier have been married for 15 years now, and their four children range in age from 7 to 17. After staying at home while the kids were small, Natalia was eager to start a new business when the youngest began kindergarten. She attended a couple of franchise shows but nothing wowed her. She knew that she needed to find a business with great income potential that would still allow her to be home for the kids.

Then she heard through a friend that a local gift-basket franchise was being sold. Nat met with the current owner of the franchise to find out more and loved what she heard. The franchise had a strong network of clients, and the parent company provided great support and product for the baskets. The current owner was selling because her family was moving to the east coast, and she was looking for just the right person to take over the business.

Nat went home that night and talked it over with Javier. The next day she contacted the current owner to find out how to begin the purchase process. In two weeks, she was flying out to British Columbia to meet the founders of the company, and by the time she returned to Ottawa, she had an offer being prepared by her agent. That was three years ago.

Nat has since built her gift-basket business into one of the most successful franchises in the chain. She has devoted herself to creating a solid stream of income that will help her family accomplish their goals, which include ensuring the kids are able to play sports and take music lessons, the family can take a vacation every year, and she and her husband can put aside money toward their retirement. She loves creating financial security for herself and her family.

This strategy and devotion paid off when Javier was laid off from his tech job in Kanata six months ago. He received a decent severance package and, in consultation with Nat and their team of advisors, including an accountant and myself, he came up with a plan for his next career move. Three months ago, Javier started his own business as an IT consultant. His first client? His wife. He took a loan from Natalia to cover his business start-up costs, using a contract they had their lawyer draft and their accountant approve, and then he signed another contract to provide IT services to her rapidly expanding business.

He is currently building a software system that will manage her customers and leads to make sure her marketing is working as efficiently as possible. He has also taken on the responsibility of data entry and database maintenance, tasks that Nat is thrilled to give up. Because he is a contractor, he can write off the part of their home where he does his work, as well as his cellphone and other expenses, against his income. Javier is actively seeking other clients, and the plan is to replace his previous salary within the next two years.

This change has allowed Javier and Natalia to spend much more time with each other and with their kids. Their overall income has dropped quite a bit with the loss of Javier's salary, but their quality of life has increased tremendously, and we have adjusted their financial plan so that they are still moving toward their goals. When Javier worked in Kanata, he rarely saw his children, especially the youngest, who often went to bed before he got home. Now, he is there when they get back from school and can attend their games and recitals. His work for Natalia has also made it feel much more like a family business. In fact, their oldest son saw Dad working for Mom and figured he might as well get a job, too. He now helps Nat with packaging, has shown a flair for design, and is planning to apply to an art and design college in Ottawa.

Natalia and Javier's successful income-splitting strategy has reduced their overall tax bill and ensured that they get through a period of reduced income without having to touch their retirement savings. They also love that more of the money her business earns is staying in the family. Their financial plan is constantly evolving as their situation changes, but it looks like a rosy future for this "gifted" family!

Chapter Summary

Make sure to get a comprehensive financial plan to save thousands of dollars in taxes:

- Shift income from high-earning years to low-earning years.
- Maximize your tax credits.
- Remember, tax deductions still cost you money.
- Use RRSPs in high-income years.
- Use TFSAs in low-income years.
- Consider withdrawing money from your RRSP in low-income years.
- Consider splitting income with your spouse if he or she earns a much lower income.
- Keep interest income sheltered in RRSPs or TFSAs.
- Keep dividend income outside of RRSPs or TFSAs.
- Retirement tax planning:
  - Must have a comprehensive financial plan.
  - Your plan should level out taxable income through retirement.
  - Start RRSP withdrawals early.

- ◦ Consider larger withdrawals prior to 65/67 and the start of Old Age Security.
- ◦ Use TFSAs to supplement income and avoid clawback of Old Age Security.
- ◦ Consider using spousal RRSPs to optimize income-splitting prior to 65.
- ◦ Base RRIF withdrawals on the younger spouse's age.
- ◦ Split pension and RRIF income with your spouse.
- ◦ Assign (split) CPP credits with your spouse.
- Shelter excess assets that you will never use by:
  - ◦ Contributing to TFSAs (yours, your children's, or your grandchildren's).
  - ◦ Purchasing permanent insurance policies.
  - ◦ Giving money away to heirs.
  - ◦ Paying down mortgages on principal residences (yours, your children's, and possibly your grandchildren's).

FOUR

ENSURING FINANCIAL SUCCESS

11

WILLS, POWERS OF ATTORNEY, AND PERSONAL CARE DIRECTIVES

A son can bear with equanimity the loss of his father, but the loss of his inheritance may drive him to despair.

—*Niccolo Machiavelli*

CONGRATULATIONS ON MAKING IT TO this point in the book! Now that you've been through all these steps to get your finances in order, it would be a shame for them to end up going to the wrong people or being controlled by a government-appointed trustee. It is for these reasons that wills, powers of attorney, and personal care directives are a critical component of financial success.

Whether you are single or married, widowed or divorced, have children or not, these three documents can play an important role in ensuring that your wishes are followed when it comes to your assets during life and upon your death, and your personal care.

From this chapter you will get an understanding of what the different documents are for and what they're capable of doing for you and for your family and heirs. It will explain the main components of each of these documents and the people who will need to be considered before preparing them.

With the information provided within this chapter, you should be able to determine a number of the factors necessary to have these documents prepared for you by a professional. By having all of this information up front and combined with all the work you have done on your finances to this point and understanding what's involved, this information could save you several hundred dollars in legal fees as a lawyer will not need to spend the time taking you through every step in the process.

This chapter in no way means to provide you with legal advice. It is solely to help you understand what's involved and to start thinking about how you would like your assets and affairs managed. I strongly recommend that you work with a lawyer who specializes in wills and estates to help you prepare a comprehensive will, power of attorney, and personal care directive. Understand that each province has its own legislation governing each of these documents. It is important to work with a professional in your province to ensure that the documents are drawn up properly.

Professional Lawyers vs. Will Kits

It is important for you to have these documents. If you are in a very tight financial situation, you can purchase software to prepare your own will, power of attorney, and personal care directive, but these are very limited in their ability to assess your unique financial and family situation. Although they can create a legally valid will, they cannot provide you with the personalized advice that can be so critical in these situations. I would strongly suggest you find a lawyer who can help you prepare your will, power of attorney, and personal care directive rather than using one of the software packages. If you use the software, you may open your will and your wishes to attack from other parties—possibly even from family. As well, there's a possibility that you'll end up with a much larger income tax and estate tax bill, having not worked with a professional advisor to coach you on the best way to structure and set up these documents.

One Frank Thought

If the cost of having these documents properly prepared for you by a lawyer (approximately $1,000) is too much, then definitely purchase one of these software packages, prepare the document, and have it signed and witnessed. I would rather you have something that explains your wishes than not have anything at all.

The Value of Naming a Contingent Individual

When preparing these three documents, you will need to choose individuals to help execute your wishes, as well as individuals you want to receive the proceeds of your assets. It is wise to name contingent individuals to succeed the primary individual you wish to manage your affairs. This way, if something should happen to the primary individual, it is not left to a court to decide who will manage your assets or affairs.

Wills

A will is a legal document that expresses your wishes about what should happen to your assets after you die. By preparing a will, you have the ability to control how your property is distributed after you die. You also have an opportunity to name a personal representative or executor or trustee who will be responsible for carrying out the directions of your will. To prepare a legal will, you must be of sound mind and of legal age, typically 18.

Dying Intestate: If you die without a will, you are said to have died intestate. In these situations, provincial intestacy laws govern how your assets are distributed. Most provinces have a succession table that shows who will receive the proceeds of your estate. For example, this may mean that the first $200,000 of your estate goes to your spouse and the remainder is equally distributed among your spouse and your children. If you don't have a spouse or children, then your estate may go to your siblings. If you don't have any siblings, it may go to your parents. If you have no successive heirs, then, and only then, your assets will go to the government.

English Form Will: This is the most common type of will in Canada. It is recognized in all provinces. It is usually typed. It must be signed in front of two witnesses, who also sign the document. Witnesses cannot be beneficiaries.

Notarial Will: Valid only in the province of Quebec, this type of will is more about the process than the format. First, you prepare a will and then you bring it to a notary. The notary reads your will to you in the presence of two other notaries. You then sign the will in front of the notary; the other two notaries sign as witnesses. The notary keeps an original copy.

One Frank Thought

I personally believe notarial wills to be the most efficient and effective way of preparing wills. A notary stamps the document, officially recognizes it as your will, and registers it, so you never need worry about it being lost or altered because it is recorded in the database. This helps with faster settlement of estates without the need for probate, and it helps to ensure your wishes are carried out. These factors can be a huge advantage during a time when there is often much uncertainty.

If You Are Married

Many couples create what are called mirrored wills: you leave everything to your spouse, and your spouse leaves everything to you. Although this makes it very clean, simple, and efficient in the transition of an estate, when it comes to special family situations (primarily blended families), it can create problems and confusion on the passing of the second spouse. For example, if both you and your spouse have your own children and you also have children together, after you've passed away your spouse could take the entire value of your estate and pass it solely to his or her children, and your children from your other partner could be left with nothing. In these situations, it may be best to set up trusts for your children. See the section on trusts further down.

Common Disaster Clause

Many wills have a clause stipulating that, in the event that you and your spouse pass away at the same time, the estate goes to another beneficiary. Many of these statements go one step further and state that if your spouse does not survive you by at least 30 days (this is a common time frame), then the balance of the estate goes to your successive beneficiaries. This 30-day time frame can force a delay in the transition and distribution of your estate as nothing can be done with it until this time frame has expired.

Choosing an Executor/Personal Representative/Trustee

An executor is an individual who you choose to manage your estate according to your will. This job can be very complex and can require a lot of work. The person you choose must be willing and able to manage your affairs on your behalf. Some of the duties of an executor include:

- Applying for the death certificate and arranging for the funeral.
- Locating important documents; managing necessary expenses, such as mortgage payments, property taxes, utility bills, funeral expenses, and medical bills; and cancelling memberships and subscriptions, etc.
- Locating and determining the existence of insurance policies and investment assets.
- Initiating the probate of the will.
- Communicating with the beneficiaries about the progress of the distribution of the estate.
- Disposing of any household and personal goods that have not been left to anyone.

Your executor should be someone who:

- Is capable of managing your assets and estate and has some good business sense.
- Lives in the same province or territory as you and your assets.
- You trust.
- Is in good health and who you expect to survive you.

Your executor can be:

- A friend or acquaintance.
- A trust company hired to act as your executor.
- Your spouse or other relative.
- A beneficiary named in your will.

When naming an executor, it is best to name only one individual, as many decisions need to be made by an executor, and to require constant communication between two or more people, plus duplicate documentation and signatures, can double the executor's work. That said, it can be beneficial to name a professional trust company as a co-executor to help your executor deal with the multitude of documentation and formalities required in dealing with the transition of your estate. While the trust company deals with all the formalities, your executor can keep an eye out and make sure that your interests and the interests of your beneficiaries are protected.

Ensure that you name an alternate executor in case your primary executor is unable to fulfill his or her duties. If there is no executor named or no successive executor available to perform the duties, the jurisdictional court will appoint an agent to act as executor on behalf of your estate.

One Frank Thought

You would be wise to prepare a letter to your executor explaining some of the details of your will. This can help your executor to understand in more detail, and with less legal language, what it is that you are trying to do. You can also offer a memorandum to explain why you left certain items or amounts to one person and certain items and amounts to another person or why you left somebody out altogether. Although this document is not binding on the executor, it can make his or her life much easier if he or she understands what your wishes are when it comes to distribution and management of your estate.

See the checklist for choosing an executor at www.howtoeatanelephant.ca.

Choosing a Guardian

If you have children under the age of majority, you should select one or more guardians for them and name those guardians in your will. If both parents of a child pass away while the child is still a minor, a guardian must be appointed to care for the child. Interestingly, the courts don't have to accept the person named in the will, but it does carry considerable weight. In most circumstances the judge will appoint the person you have named as long as it is in the best interests of the child.

Until your children reach the age of majority, your guardian's job will be to act as the legally responsible adult for the children and provide the best caregiving arrangements possible for your children's circumstances.

Your guardian must be:

- Over the age of majority.
- Familiar with your family and the child or children whom they will care for.
- In good health and young enough to care for the children.
- Able to make decisions about raising the children consistent with your values and beliefs.
- Able to provide a home environment for your children consistent with your wishes.

This person does not have to be the same for all children, and the guardian can also be your executor, a beneficiary, or a relative. Most people choose their spouse to be the primary guardian, but in the event of a common disaster (where both you and your spouse pass away at the same time), you should name an alternative.

It is best to name only one individual as the guardian, rather than naming a couple. The reason for this is that should the couple split up, the courts would decide who should take care of the child.

You can advise the executor to use the financial resources left to your children for the children's maintenance, as deemed reasonable by the executor. This should help to alleviate some of the financial burden the guardian may face in raising your children.

One Frank Thought

As with your executor, it may be wise to write a letter to be given to your children's guardian at the time of your death that explains your wishes and desires for raising your children, as well as your children's pertinent history and medical information. This letter could be as simple as one page, or it could be a small book in which you share your thoughts, goals, and dreams for your children. Although not a legal document, and although the guardian has no obligation to follow your wishes, many feel this is helpful to both guardian and children during a very difficult transition.

See the checklist for choosing a guardian online at www.howtoeatan elephant.ca.

Distributing Your Estate

When you think about the distribution of your estate, you need to consider in what manner you will distribute the assets. You can name specific people to receive specific assets, or you can simply divide up your estate and have individuals receive a percentage. Let's take a look at both of these options and the pros and cons of each.

Specific Gifts

Specific gifts are useful when used in combination with leaving the residue of your estate to specific beneficiaries. For example, you may want to leave a specific sum of money to an individual whom you do not wish to leave the residue of your estate to, such as a charity or community organization. Another example may be that you wish to leave specific shares that have a large capital gain to a charity to avoid the capital gains tax. Or you may have promised a specific item to a specific family member and wish to ensure that he or she receives it.

The reasons you may not want to leave specific gifts in your will include:

- That the item might no longer exist at the time of your death.
- The value of the item might have changed considerably by the time you die.
- The beneficiary of the specific item might not be alive at the time of your death.
- The asset is jointly owned and may not form part of your estate and cannot be governed by your will.

You can always provide your executor with a memorandum explaining that you wish specific assets to go to specific people through a residue distribution rather than specific gift declarations. This can be beneficial as you can update this memorandum at any time without having to redo your will. Although this memorandum is not a legal document, it does provide guidance to your executor in following your wishes.

Not specifying items for specific beneficiaries allows your executor to use his or her discretion to make sure the division of gifts is equitable given what assets are left at the time of your death.

One Frank Thought

If you are using specific gifts to distribute your assets, you would be wise to use the term "net value" of the gift so that the estate does not end up having to pay the tax bill of the gift.

Another way to distribute specific assets is to do so during your lifetime. This can have many advantages, but you need to be sure not to distribute so much that you run into financial hardship. You get to see your beneficiaries using the assets while you are still alive, and it can also reduce your lifetime tax bill. You may choose to donate money to a charity while you are still alive, thereby benefitting from the tax credit that is generated through the donation.

One Frank Thought

There are many ways you can gift specific assets to individuals. These each create different tax liabilities, credits, and deductions. For this reason, should you decide to make specific gifts of assets, it should be done with the help of a certified financial planner or tax expert in estate planning who can provide you with the advice and guidance to do this most efficiently.

Distributing Your Estate through Residue

The residue of your estate is defined as the property remaining in the estate after all debts and obligations, including funeral expenses, have been paid off and after all specific gifts or bequests have been fulfilled. For many reasons, this can be a very efficient, simple, flexible, and effective way to distribute your estate to those whom you wish to receive it. One problem that arises is that we never know exactly how much of our estate will be left for distribution through residue. This is why it is important to have a residue clause in your will even if you plan to specifically gift all assets.

If you have more than a single beneficiary, you should specify the distribution of your estate in percentage terms. A common format would be to divide the estate into 100 shares and specify how many shares you would like each beneficiary to receive. If you wish one beneficiary to receive 20% of the residue, then you would issue them 20 shares through your estate.

The taxes of your estate will be paid out of the residue, even the taxes generated by gifts that are not included in the estate or its residue. When there are not enough funds in the residue to pay the taxes on the estate, specific gifts will have to be liquidated to pay the taxes

It is important to ensure that you make adequate provision for your spouse and legal dependents in your will, based on the legislation in your jurisdiction. If you fail to provide adequate funds for your dependents, they have the opportunity to apply to the courts under dependent-relief legislation to instruct the estate to pay a fair and reasonable amount for their support.

Naming Beneficiary Designations

As you're preparing your will, power of attorney, and personal care directive, you should take a few minutes to review any beneficiary designations that exist on your life insurance policies, investment accounts, retirement savings plans, pensions, and other investment assets. I often meet people who have beneficiaries named on these documents to whom they are no longer married and to whom they wish no assets to go. One of the most common beneficiary designations (as it is the default on many accounts) is the person's estate, but this can cause substantial tax liability to your estate.

Through the simple process of filling out paperwork on your accounts, pensions, and life insurance policies, you can name one or more individuals as beneficiaries of these specific accounts or policies. This ensures that the assets pass outside of your estate, avoiding probate and going directly to those whom you wish to have them, without delay or challenge from other beneficiaries or creditors. This does not avoid, but may delay, any tax liability that results from the disposition and transfer of assets to the beneficiary.

You should be aware that by naming beneficiaries on these accounts, these assets will not form part of your estate and, therefore, are not governed by your will. This means that anything in your will pertaining to those accounts will not have power and will not take effect. In circumstances where the beneficiary named on an account has predeceased you, you can, through your will, name a contingent beneficiary.

Who Should You Name as Designated Beneficiary on Non-Registered Investment Accounts?

An ideal choice is to name minor children in trust. You can then name your spouse (or other guardian of the children) to be the trustee so that they can control the assets and use them to support the children. This allows the income generated by the investment account to be taxed in the children's hands, as well as the hands of the trust, thereby reducing the overall taxes that have to be paid on those assets—a process similar to income-splitting. If you named your spouse or the guardian as the direct beneficiary, then the assets would be taxed at his or her (likely) higher tax rate.

Who Should You Name as Designated Beneficiary on RRSP Investment Accounts?

You should almost always name your spouse as the beneficiary of your RRSP to allow for the tax-free rollover of those assets into your spouse's RRSP. In the event that your spouse has predeceased you or that you do not have a spouse at the time of your death, then naming a disabled dependent would allow you to accomplish a similar type of rollover. If you do not have a disabled dependent, then naming a minor child can also help defer the tax liability on the RRSP.

One Frank Thought

Even if you can't take advantage of a tax rollover, it is still worth naming a designated beneficiary so that the assets pass outside the estate. This helps to reduce probate fees and the delay caused by having to probate an estate. Remember, though, that your estate will have to pay the tax bill generated by these registered assets even though your designated beneficiary may receive the entire amount pre-tax. This can create a large tax burden for your estate and possibly for other beneficiaries.

Who Should You Name as Designated Beneficiary of Your Life Insurance Policies?

As the payouts on life insurance policies are tax-free, many people don't think about the tax consequence to the beneficiary that results from investing the proceeds of life insurance. This can, in many circumstances, generate significant annual income that can create a significant tax bill for the beneficiary. To help reduce that tax bill, it may be best to leave the insurance proceeds to the beneficiary in trust. This creates another taxable entity (the trust) that can claim some or all of the income and that income can be taxed in the hands of the trust. This effectively creates an income-splitting opportunity.

For example, let's say you leave your spouse $1 million in insurance proceeds, which generates a return of 5%. He or she currently earns $100,000 from employment income, so the income earned from the insurance proceeds will end up being taxed at approximately 43%. If you leave it in trust to your spouse, then the money can be invested within the trust and that same 5% interest can be held and taxed within the trust before being distributed to your spouse. This would likely see the income taxed at approximately 23%.

One Frank Thought

If the trust earns eligible dividends, which are then taxed in the hands of the trust, they won't qualify for the dividend tax credit, thereby reducing the tax-effectiveness of this income. It may make sense to flow the dividend income through to your spouse or beneficiary so they may claim the dividend tax credit.

Trusts for Minor Children

It is important when preparing your will to have your minor children taken care of. Many minor children are not able to manage large sums of money or assets, even as they become young adults. It is best to set up a testamentary trust for your children, with your spouse or other guardian named as the trustee. The trustee can use the funds to raise and take care of the children. Through this trust, you have the opportunity to dictate when the children may access the funds and how much money they have access to. This can be useful to help children learn basic money-management skills without putting large sums of money into their hands at an early age. By setting up the trust so that they receive portions of the money over time, they can learn how to handle the money and use it to help pay for school, buy their first house, or maybe start their own business. It is important to allow the trustee to encroach on the capital as they see fit to take care of the children and pay for the children's expenses.

One Frank Thought

My wife and I have set up our trust so that each of our children will receive a lump sum of $200,000 at the age of majority. This should be more than enough for them to pay for school, purchase a car, and have some money left for spending. It should also help them learn how to manage money. We then allow them to take one-third of the value of their trust at ages 24, 28, and 30. This will give them the funds to purchase their first house and get them started in life, without the fear that they will receive a large lump sum all at once and waste it or have it taken from them. Having a trustee managing the assets and providing guidance and advice to ensure that they are well taken care of adds a layer of comfort.

Powers of Attorney

This document is also now known as an "enduring power of attorney" or, in Ontario, as a "continuing power of attorney." These legal documents give authority to a named individual to act as your representative on financial decisions while you are still alive.

There are two types of powers of attorney: immediate and springing. With an immediate power of attorney, your named representative has the power to make financial decisions on your behalf as soon as the document is signed and witnessed. With the springing power of attorney, your named representative's power only comes into effect once you've been declared in writing by two doctors to be mentally incompetent to make financial decisions on your own. All enduring powers of attorney terminate when you die. Upon your death, your executor takes over. Your representative does not have the authority to make decisions about your health; for that, you should prepare a personal care directive.

The reason these documents are so critical to financial success is that, without them, should you become incapacitated and unable to manage your financial affairs, your business and investment assets could get into real trouble. Without this document, it could take months, or even years, for the courts to appoint another person to take charge of your financial affairs. Without a power of attorney, a family member or other person must make an application to the court to be appointed your representative. In some circumstances, the court may appoint a public trustee to manage your assets and protect your rights.

Responsibilities of Your Attorney

Your representative will be responsible for:

- Filing your tax returns
- Managing your investments
- Managing all your financial obligations, debts, and ongoing living and personal maintenance costs
- Using your assets to provide support for your dependents

- Providing a detailed accounting of your assets to the courts, if required

The responsibility of being someone's attorney can last for months or even years. Therefore, when choosing an attorney, ensure that he or she is:

- Trustworthy
- In good health
- Available and able to manage your finances
- Likely to survive you
- Aware that you've selected him or her to be your attorney
- Familiar with you, your family, and your financial situation
- Living near you, preferably in the same province or territory

Your attorney can be:

- A friend or acquaintance
- A trust company hired to act as an attorney
- A lawyer or trusted advisor
- Your spouse or relative

Being an attorney can involve quite a lot of work and take a lot of time. Although the perception that you are smart and intelligent enough to manage the affairs on behalf of someone else may be honourable, the amount of work involved can be burdensome. This being the case, the attorney is entitled to compensation, and each province and territory has legislation outlining acceptable compensation.

See the checklist for choosing a power of attorney online at www.howto eatanelephant.ca.

Personal Care Directives

Otherwise known as "powers of attorney for personal care," "advanced healthcare directives," or "living wills," these legal documents help your appointed representative or attorney make decisions about your personal health care when you are unable to do so. These documents give you an opportunity to explain your wishes about how you should be treated and what forms of treatment should be performed. These are known as "proxy directives," and they let you give someone else the authority, or proxy, to make the decisions for you.

A personal care directive can address issues beyond medical consent. You can also use it to express how you would like to have your personal care, health care, and other non-financial personal matters dealt with, should you not have the capacity to make your own decisions.

One Frank Thought

Not all jurisdictions have legislation authorizing these documents, but when the court in one of those jurisdictions has to make a decision, a personal care directive can help to show what your wishes were at the time of signing. Although the court does not have to follow your wishes, the document will carry a fair bit of weight.

When you choose someone to be your personal care representative, you are asking them to take on a large responsibility. When preparing this document, you can do your representative a great favour by outlining what you would like to see happen. This document can go a long way toward making it simple for your representative to follow your instructions about personal care.

The decisions that your personal care representative might need to make on your behalf include:

- The kind of medical treatment and medication you should receive
- First instructions regarding your personal care to medical staff
- Information and instruction regarding your ongoing health care
- Whether you should be looked after at home or in an institution
- The kind of food you should be eating
- How to deal with various non-financial personal matters
- If and when you should be removed from life support

One Frank Thought

As with the other documents mentioned in this chapter, it may be wise to prepare a letter that goes along with your personal care directive that explains your thoughts and wishes in detail using simple language. This can go a long way in explaining, not just to your personal representative, but to your family as well, why you've made the decisions you have.

As the role of personal care representative may last for months, years, and sometimes decades, your representative should be:

- Over the age of majority
- Living near you
- Trustworthy
- Familiar with you, your family, and your personal lifestyle
- In good health and likely to survive you
- Able to make time to deal with your personal health care decisions
- Asked to be your representative and agreed

Your representative can be a spouse, relative, friend, or acquaintance.

One Frank Thought

If you would really like to appoint a family member to make decisions about your personal care, but he or she does not live anywhere near you, consider appointing two people as personal care representatives. One can be a friend or acquaintance who lives nearby, and one can be a family member who lives further away. The friend or acquaintance can interact with the medical professionals and communicate with the family member who is further away.

Most people name their spouse as their representative. While being your personal care representative is a big responsibility, it is likely your spouse would be involved in your personal care decisions anyway.

Although it is unpleasant to contemplate losing your life, falling critically ill, or becoming disabled, planning ahead for these events not only helps you and your family, but also is the responsible thing to do. Wills, powers of attorney, and personal care directives are critical components of a sound financial plan. It would be a shame if the finances you've worked so hard to get into shape were ruined because you did not prepare these documents.

One Frank Thought

I would be remiss if I didn't encourage you to have an open discussion about your wishes with those who are involved. When preparing your will, it is a good idea to sit down with your family and explain to them what your wishes are and have an open and honest discussion about their thoughts and feelings. This is also a good idea when it comes to personal care directives and powers of attorney. These conversations may help you gain a better understanding of how your family members feel and what they would like to see happen when it comes to your well-being and assets. Some clients of mine had originally planned to leave the majority of their assets to their children. But when they sat down and talked to them about it, the kids said that they didn't need the assets nor did they really want them. My clients were able to change their wills so that more of the assets went to charity, and the remainder went into a trust for their grandchildren, bypassing their children entirely.

See the checklist for choosing a personal care representative online at www.howtoeatanelephant.ca.

Samuel and Lea

Samuel and Lea met at a business conference seven years ago and sparks flew immediately. They married within a year and moved into Sam's home in Niagara Falls, where his truck-parts manufacturing facility was located. His eldest child, Deborah, questioned why her 60-year-old father would marry a woman half his age with two small children.

Sam sighed when he explained that, although his daughter refused to believe he was in love with Lea and her little girls, he was happy to have children's laughter in the house again, and they made him feel young.

Having run a successful manufacturing business for 25 years, Sam was an expert at assembling the right team of advisors, and he gathered them to update his estate documents. Deborah was being groomed to run the business when he retired and Sam, being the consummate planner that he was, moved to head off any potential trouble by making changes to his will and powers of attorney to include Lea and the girls.

Sam and Lea enjoyed one fantastic year together, and then Sam was diagnosed with a malignant brain tumour. In the chaos of a rapidly progressing disease, his legal documents proved their value again and again. The tumour was plum-sized when it was diagnosed and removal seemed the only option. The surgery was a success, and Sam stayed in rehab for three months while his short-term memory returned and he underwent radiation treatments. Lea visited him every day, even though some days he couldn't remember who she was. After rehab, he returned home with nursing care to continue his recovery.

During this time, Deborah ran the plant, proving that she knew the operations and supply chains inside and out. Sam's power of attorney and personal care directive were both in effect during this period, as he was incapable of making decisions. His most senior outside counsel became his overseeing attorney, who ensured that his wishes were carried out: his children had the power they needed to run the company, and Lea and her girls received support.

Just as Sam was beginning to act like Sam again, he had a fatal stroke. Doctors thought that perhaps it had been caused by bleeding from the surgery or radiation, but to Lea and his family it hardly mattered. All they knew was that their husband and father was gone, and they were left in this strange family dynamic with people they barely knew. Often a common tragedy will bring people together but, unfortunately, this was not what happened in Lea's case. Deborah turned her grief into anger and demanded that Lea move out of her father's home.

Lea was fortunate that Sam had acted so decisively with his legal documents. His executor, the same man who had acted as his attorney during his illness, became Lea's defender. Sam's will was specific about how his estate was to be divided, and each of his three children received large lump-sum inheritances and precious family heirlooms. Deborah and her youngest brother, Danny, were given controlling interest in the business. Lea was given the home, Sam's RRSP, 50% of the proceeds from a life insurance policy on which she was a named beneficiary, and a 20% interest in his business. He had ensured that she would never have to worry about money again.

Sam had also taken out a key person life insurance policy many years ago. This policy paid the business a lump sum on his death.

Deborah was furious, and she and Danny launched a lawsuit to contest the will. It took almost three years to progress through the courts. Lea remained in the home with her girls and their expenses were paid by Sam's estate. After losing in a lower court, Deborah took the case to appeal.

The appeal was denied, the ruling was upheld, and Sam's children were ordered to pay Lea's legal fees. They were unable to prove their argument that Sam must have been under the influence of the tumour when he had written the will—and married Lea, for that matter. The defence had presented a clean bill of health from his annual physical shortly before the will was written, as well as the testimony of his team of advisors. The case was a sad finale to the life of a great man, and we remained hopeful that his children would realize the damage the lawsuit was doing to their own interests in the estate, as well as to their health and happiness. Lea sold the house in Niagara, and the business bought back her ownership with the proceeds from the key person policy. Lea moved back to Newfoundland to be closer to her family and to get away from the hurtful memories of Sam's family.

Théo and Chloé

Théo and Chloé moved from New Brunswick to Red Deer several years ago to take advantage of the oil boom. Companies were desperately in need of employees and, having just graduated from a

Resource Management program, both Théo and Chloé had skills that oil field-service companies were looking for. Théo travels quite a lot around the province, doing environmental assessments to satisfy government regulations, while Chloé maintains the resource-mapping system at another company. Overall, their income is just over $150,000 before taxes.

Théo has been waiting for Chloé to be ready to have a baby since their wedding five years ago, and several months ago she announced that she was ready. A few days later, they gave me a call to evaluate how a child would impact their current financial plan and to rejig their budget in anticipation of a reduced income and increased expenses. I gave them a checklist to help them prepare, and they started to work through it.

A few weeks after that, they called back to ask about the legal documents. Théo asked me if they really needed to worry about the wills and powers of attorney at this point. He said, "But we're so young!" Many people allow fear and a lack of understanding to keep them from undertaking proper planning, and it can have disastrous consequences, especially for parents with young children.

I told him about a 35-year-old man who had been in an industrial accident. He was in the hospital for just over six months, and, if he had not had a power of attorney, it would have been very difficult for his wife to access his accounts and take care of their household expenses. I assured him that when it came to planning, being prepared was always better than leaving things to chance and wishing for the best. Being young is no reason not to plan. In fact, the earlier people start to plan, the easier it is to achieve their goals and the lifestyle they desire.

I worked with them as they carefully determined the details of their will and life insurance policies. They designated each other as primary beneficiaries on their RRSPs and insurance policies to ensure that if anything happened to one of them, the surviving spouse and any children would be protected. They also explained in their wills that any children should be the beneficiaries if both parents should die, with the estate proceeds to be held in trust for those under 18. After talking it over with their families, they named Chloé's sister as the guardian for any children they might have.

Finally, they worked out their powers of attorney and personal care directives to ensure that there would be no financial difficulties if one of them was incapacitated.

When they called to tell me that they were finished, about three months ago, I congratulated them on taking care of such an important component of their financial plan and stressed to them how important it was to review their wills as their lives and financial circumstances changed. While none of us like to think about the bad that might happen, if we are properly prepared, we can respond in much healthier ways, knowing that we are taken care of. Chloé sent me an email recently to let me know that they are expecting a child in six months! Helping people get on top of their lives, at all stages of life, is one of the best parts of this job.

Chapter Summary

- Work with a legal professional to help you prepare documents.
- If you can't afford to work with a professional, purchase a software kit to prepare these documents.
- Download the checklists for these documents at www.howtoeatan elephant.ca.
- Wills:
  - Choose an executor and an alternative executor for your will and estate.
  - Speak with them about the duties and responsibilities involved.
  - Prepare a letter to your executor explaining your wishes.
  - Choose a guardian for minor children, along with an alternate.
  - Consider limiting specific gifts.
  - Be sure to understand the tax implications of specific gifts.
  - Ensure you have a residue clause.
  - Ensure you provide adequately for your spouse and any dependents
  - Consider leaving assets in trust to create an income-splitting opportunity.

- Create trusts for minor or young children to help manage a large inheritance.
- Review all beneficiary designations on investment accounts and/ or life insurance policies.
- Powers of Attorney:
  - Choose an attorney and an alternate to manage your affairs when you can't.
  - Speak to your chosen attorney or alternate to ensure they understand what their responsibilities are.
  - Prepare a letter to your attorney to explain what they need to do.
  - Attorneys cannot make decisions on health issues.
  - Understand that this responsibility may last a long time.
- Personal Care Directives:
  - Choose a representative and an alternate to make decisions around your healthcare and personal care when you can't.
  - Speak to both your representative and alternate to ensure they understand what their responsibilities are and that they are willing to take on those responsibilities.
  - Prepare letters explaining how you would like to be taken care of.
  - Consider appointing more than one person if the location and proximity to you will be an issue.
- Keep a copy of these documents in a safe place.
- Share a copy of these documents with your executor, attorney, or personal care representative.

How To Eat An Elephant.ca—Web Tools

Wills, Powers of Attorney, and Personal Care Directives Tool

This tool helps you to identify different aspects of your personal financial situation that may need to be addressed when preparing these critical documents. If you have a spouse, it is wise to go through the questions and statements of this tool together.

> **STEP ONE:** Log into www.howtoeatanelephant.ca and select the **Wills, Powers of Attorney, and Personal Care Directives Tool** from the menu page.
>
> **STEP TWO:** Go through the statements for each of these documents and select the appropriate box if the statement applies to you and/or your spouse.
>
> **STEP THREE:** Once you are confident you have selected all that apply, click the Get Report button.
>
> **STEP FOUR:** Here you are presented with your report, which you can download and print as a PDF document.

This report lists each of the statements or questions for you and for your spouse with a space below for you to write in your thoughts and wishes. This report is not meant to provide legal advice in any way. It is meant to help reduce the time you need to spend with a lawyer preparing these documents, and to give you a greater understanding of what you might want to include in these documents.

12

FINDING THE RIGHT ADVISORS

To accept good advice is but to increase one's own ability.
—Johann Wolfgang von Goethe

CONGRATULATIONS ON GETTING TO THE final chapter of this book! By now you likely have greater confidence in your personal finances and a greater understanding of where you are and how you're going to get to where you want to be.

I would love to be able to tell you that you no longer need to worry about or deal with your personal finances going forward. The reality is, however, that personal finances are an ever-changing, ongoing matter that you will need to deal with on a regular basis.

I hope you found this book and its exercises to be enlightening and manageable. Personal finance does not need to be a difficult or scary thing. As you move forward, you may choose not to do this alone. I would strongly encourage you to continue your education through the many resources that are available. I would also recommend that you seek out and find quality advisors to help you continue toward further financial success.

In this chapter I will help you to consider the following information when selecting a financial advisor:

- The different types of advisors out there
- The types of designations they may have

- The places you can go to find advisors
- How to select an advisor
- Recommendations for selecting the best advisor

Types of Financial Advisors

It is important to find advisors who have the relevant knowledge and experience to help you in the areas you need assistance with. For example, you may need an investment advisor to help you with investments or a financial planner to prepare your financial plan. Maybe you will also need a tax accountant to help you with taxes and a lawyer to help you with wills, businesses and corporations, or setting up trusts. Some advisors will have a combination of expertise within these different areas. Many financial planners will also be able to help with investments, tax or insurance advice, for example.

Here are some of the types of advisors, along with the variety of businesses they run, and notes about how they are compensated.

Bank Branch Financial Advisors

These financial advisors are hired by the banks to manage their banking clients' day-to-day financial needs. They typically have a limited amount of time they can work with you—maybe an hour or two—to address your immediate needs and possibly refer you to someone else within the bank to help in other areas. Generally, they are restricted to offering you the bank's products, such as mortgages, GICs, and mutual funds. These advisors are paid a nominal salary, tend to be younger and less experienced, and often change frequently as they have aspirations of promotion and moving on to bigger and better things.

Mutual Fund Sales Representatives

Mutual fund advisors are almost always commissioned salespeople who need only minimal knowledge and no experience. Although some of these advisors may have greater knowledge and experience, only a select few provide additional advice and services. Common job titles include investment advisor, financial advisor, financial planner, and financial agent. Depending on the company they work for, they may also be insurance agents.

These advisors may have many designations but are typically licensed only to offer mutual funds. Many insurance agents who work for large insurance companies are restricted to offering only segregated funds.

Brokers/Investment Advisors

These advisors typically work for brokerage firms strictly on a commission basis. Their commissions may be derived from charges on individual trades, or a flat fee as a percentage of the overall assets that they are managing. These advisors are licensed through the provincial security commission and can purchase any investment in the market for their clients. Many brokers purchase individual stocks and bonds, as well as exchange-traded funds, index units, and mutual funds. These advisors tend to have more knowledge but not necessarily more experience.

Private Client Management

These are fairly new groups set up within brokerage firms to create a brand so that they can attract high-net-worth clients. These groups tend to offer a much higher level of service, and the advisors who work there tend to have greater education, knowledge, and experience. They are positioned to provide services above and beyond investment management and tend to focus on the day-to-day management of an individual's wealth. From preparing financial plans to managing investments and arranging to pay utility bills, all the financial needs of the client are met by these firms. Some groups even offer concierge services to assist the clients in arranging everything from travel to dog-walking services.

The fees they charge depend on the level of service you require and tend to be higher than managing everything on your own. Many of the individuals who work in these areas are paid a combination of salary, bonuses, and sales commissions.

Investment Counsel

These firms tend to service the ultra-high-net-worth market with a minimum investment level of at least $1 million, and in some cases $5 million. Investment counsel firms manage large dollar accounts, such as trusts, foundations, pensions, and large individual accounts.

These firms usually do not have salespeople because their focus is on managing the hundreds of millions of dollars that they have in investments. These firms typically charge a flat fee as a percentage of the assets under management, and most of the money managers who work there tend to have many years of experience and a much higher level of education.

Fee-Only Financial Planning

These financial planners charge an hourly fee or a flat fee for the preparation of a financial plan for the client. These planners tend not to sell investment assets and spend their time focusing on preparing financial plans. With this kind of assistance, you can be assured that the advice you are receiving is unbiased.

Independent Financial Planners

Independent financial planners tend to work on a fee-only basis for independent firms that are not associated with financial products but may offer third-party products as solutions to your plan. By preparing a financial plan for you, they can make recommendations on the types of investments, insurance, mortgages, and estate-planning issues that may need to be addressed, without any obligation or bias toward a company's specific products.

Insurance Agents

Many of the large insurance companies hire salespeople to act as their agents to sell their insurance products. These products are typically life insurance, critical illness insurance, and long-term care and disability policies. Insurance companies also encourage their agents to sell the company's segregated funds as investment solutions for their clients. Many insurance salespeople have limited financial knowledge and experience and will almost always offer you their company's products. Paid by commission, agents have very little time to spend helping you prepare a proper plan to ensure that you have the right products and solutions.

Independent Insurance Brokers

Independent insurance brokers are salespeople who have the advantage of being able to source the entire market to find the best insurance products and solutions to meet their clients' needs. They too can offer segregated funds from any of the insurance companies. However, many have limited financial knowledge and experience and are also paid by commission.

• • •

How much money you have to invest may dictate who you can work with when it comes to the management of your investment assets. The more assets you have, the more experienced and knowledgeable an advisor you can attract. The chart below outlines where I believe your assets should be invested (as described in Chapter 9 on investing). It also shows you the best type of advisor to help you. As your assets mature, so should your advice. No matter what level your assets are at, working with a CFP to prepare a comprehensive financial plan may be the best investment you ever make.

Amount of Investment	Best Investment Option		Best Advisor to Help
$0 - $60,000	Mutual Funds		Bank or Mutual Funds Salespeople
$60,000 - $200,000	ETF and Index Units		Discount Broker
$200,000 - $500,000	Stocks and Bonds	Certified Financial Planner (CFP)	Broker Teams
$500,000 - $1 million	Stocks, Bonds, Preferred Shares		Private Client Groups, Broker Teams
$1 million +	Stocks, Bonds, Preferred Shares, Options, Partnerships …		Investment Counsel Teams

Although there are many pros and cons to each type of advisor, it is important that you understand:

- How advisors are compensated
- What limitations the advisors have in the products and services they can offer you

- How many years of relevant experience they have
- Their level of education
- Their approach and philosophy
- Whether you like them

Designations

When looking for advisors, it is important that you assess their education and accreditation levels. However, all the acronyms make it difficult—a real "alphabet soup." So what do these designations mean? Below are just a few of the designations that are used in Canada.

One Frank Thought

Many people who work in the financial services industry will have multiple designations, and the work they do does not necessarily reflect the designations they have. The reality is that you can get a designation but you don't necessarily do the work relating to that designation. Using myself as an example—I have the Canadian Investment Managers (CIM) designation, yet I don't manage any money. Many mutual fund salespeople will have designations like the CFP but all they do is sell mutual funds under the guise and promise of financial planning. To better understand what advisors do and their role, use the checklist of questions at the end of the chapter to have a conversation with them.

Financial Planning Designations

Certified Financial Planner (CFP): This is an internationally recognized designation awarded by the Financial Planning Standards Council (FPSC). CFPs are able to work with clients to prepare financial plans addressing many areas, including investments, debts, taxes, estate planning, and retirement planning. CFP professionals must have two years of experience in financial planning and meet the FPSC's standards in education, experience, examination, and ethics.

Registered Financial Planner (RFP): This designation is very similar to the CFP designation in what the holder can do. They too have significant education and a minimum of three years in financial planning experience. A registered financial planner must prepare comprehensive financial plans as their primary job requirement.

Registered Retirement Consultant (RRC): The individuals entitled to use this designation focus predominantly on retirement and estate planning.

Financial Management Advisor (FMA): A designation granted by the Canadian Securities Institute (CSI) in advanced financial planning and wealth management. Graduates of the FMA program are able to provide advanced financial-planning advice to sophisticated and high-net-worth investors.

Personal Financial Planner (PFP): This certification program, created for the bank, trust companies, and credit unions to recognize the education and experience of their employees, focuses on the fundamentals of personal finance and requires three years of relevant work experience.

Chartered Strategic Wealth Professional (CSWP): This designation focuses on learning about managing personal wealth and financial planning at a higher level for affluent Canadians.

Trust and Estate Practitioner (TEP): This international designation places strong emphasis on creating, managing, and implementing trusts, as well as advanced estate planning.

Fellow of the FPSC™: This is the highest designation in financial planning and is awarded to those who have attained the CFP designation and demonstrated a long-standing commitment to promoting financial planning.

Investment Management Designations

Chartered Financial Analyst (CFA): A tough designation to get—usually investment managers work toward this designation. Candidates must pass three levels of exams in areas including accounting, economics, ethics, money management, and security analysis. Candidates must have three years of experience and a bachelor's degree.

Canadian Investment Manager (CIM): This designation from the CSI requires candidates to complete courses in securities, investment, and portfolio management.

Fellowship of the Canadian Securities Institute (FCSI): This designation is one of the highest within the financial services industry. It requires significant education, as well as a minimum of five years of experience.

Accounting Designations

Chartered Accountant (CA): CAs are business professionals who generally work in four key areas (public practice, industry, government, or education). They provide accounting and business advice to clients. A CA has completed successfully the education, examination, and experience requirements of the Institute of Chartered Accountants. Members must adhere to a code of professional ethics/ conduct, attain mandatory continuing education, and obtain mandatory professional liability insurance with respect to any public accounting practice.

Certified General Accountant (CGA): CGAs work globally in industry, commerce, finance, government, public practice, and other areas where accounting and financial management are required. An adherence to high professional and practice standards ensures that CGAs continue to offer superior professional services worthy of the public's trust.

Certified Management Accountant (CMA): Working in organizations of all sizes and types, CMAs provide an integrated perspective to business decision-making. They have unique competencies in cost management, strategic performance measurement, process management, risk management and assurance services, and stakeholder reporting, coupled with the ability to connect strategy with operations and anticipate customer and supplier needs.

Insurance Designations

Chartered Life Underwriter (CLU): An individual who has passed exams administered by the Financial Advisors Association of

Canada (Advocis), indicating that he or she is a qualified life insurance agent.

Registered Health Underwriter (RHU): An individual who is an insurance/financial advisor with advanced knowledge in disability insurance underwriting.

One Frank Thought

There should be a direct correlation between the years of service and the number of designations that an advisor or planner has. To maintain designations and licensing, advisors are required to improve constantly through continuing education. In many cases, these can be very basic courses that will allow the advisor to qualify. However, I believe that a worthy advisor will want to go out and achieve additional accreditation. Designations can be achieved in only two or three years of continuing education. My designations include CFP, RRC, FMA, CIM, FCSI, and FELLOW OF THE FPSC™.

Choosing an Advisor

When you are ready to go out and look for an advisor to help you with your personal finances, you need to be prepared to answer some questions first. You also need to be prepared to ask a number of questions.

Build Your List

Fortunately, this book is a great guide to help you with this process. So where do you start? My recommendation to you would be to start with family and friends. Who do they currently use as their advisors? Ask them a few questions about what they like and don't like about their advisor and about the type of work the advisor does for them.

Some people may find this to be a little bit intrusive or personal, but with a simple explanation that you're not looking for specific information about their situation, they should be more than happy to share with you the information and experience they have from dealing with their advisors.

If your friends and family don't have advisors, or you don't like the ones they have, go to industry websites, such as the Financial Planning Standards Council to find a Certified Financial Planner (CFP), or the Canadian Institute of Chartered Accountants to find a chartered accountant, etc.

One Frank Thought

Be sure the advisor recommended by your family and friends works with people in your financial situation. Speak with family and friends who are in a similar financial situation to yours. Asking your rich, single, entrepreneurial uncle who he uses may not lead you to the best advisor for you and your situation.

Research the Candidates

Next, take the names and information you've collected and start to do your online research. Perform a Google search using the advisors' names and company names. Log into sites such as LinkedIn to see who they're connected to and what they're doing. Maybe you can find their profile on Facebook. They may even have a Twitter account where you can see what they've been talking about recently.

Make sure to visit the regulatory bodies' websites that govern their work to verify whether or not there have been complaints filed against them. A list of websites is provided at www.howtoeatanelephant.ca. It would also be wise to ensure that they have a licence to offer the advice and sell the products that they do.

Interview the Advisors

Once you've narrowed the list down, contact the advisors and ask to arrange a time for you to interview them. If an advisor is unwilling to spend a minimum of one hour being interviewed by you—a potential client— then he or she is not likely an advisor who would be willing to take the time to work with you on your finances.

During the interview, ask about the advisor's philosophy on how they do business and ensure that it matches your philosophy. You will also want to get a better understanding of the level of service that they will provide and the access that you will have to them, their assistant, and the company in general. Ask what total number of relevant years of experience they have. I recommend a minimum of eight to 10. Lastly, you must like the individual you select and feel that you can work with him or her.

At www.howtoeatanelephant.ca, there is a series of questions that you can take with you to advisor interviews to help you determine whether or not the advisor is a good fit for you.

One Frank Thought

When interviewing an investment advisor, you need to put yourself in the mindset that you are the boss and you are interviewing a potential employee. You need to be comfortable and confident enough to challenge the recommendations and advice given by the advisor, as well as willing to reprimand and praise the advisor for his or her work.

Ask About Compensation

To understand why an advisor may recommend one strategy or product over another, it is important to ask the following questions:

- How is the advisor compensated?
- Is he or she paid a commission or finder's fee?
- What types of products can he or she offer?
- Is he or she restricted in the various types of products that can be offered, thereby restricting the recommendations made to you about your personal financial situation?

Just asking these questions can give you a much stronger perspective and understanding about the recommendations and advice your potential advisors will provide.

Request Samples of Work Done

After interviewing several advisors (I would strongly recommend a minimum of three to five), try to narrow it down to two candidates. From the final two, request samples of client work they have completed that is relevant to your situation. The advisors should be able to remove all personal information to present to you anonymous but actual, relevant samples of work. These might be sample portfolios showing types of investments and rates of return. Also, there may be sample financial plans, tax plans, estate plans, wills, etc.

Ask for References

Once you are satisfied with this information, the final step is to ask the advisors to provide you with the names of two client references whom you can call. When speaking with the references, be sure to ask leading questions that allow them to speak about their experiences, rather than just yes or no questions. When listening to their responses, be sure to assess their tone and don't be afraid to ask for clarification.

One Frank Thought

I have always found asking for references to be a silly exercise. Why would anyone provide a reference that wasn't likely to give a glowing recommendation? It is for this reason that you want to take your time and listen to the tone and inflection of the references' responses.

By this point you should have a solid understanding of the advisors, their philosophies, levels of service, and biases, as well as an understanding of the type of information you can expect to receive. So now it's time to go out and hire yourself an employee/advisor.

Build Your Advisor Team

One individual is usually enough to provide you with advice when it comes to personal finance. You could consider hiring as many as five advisors, depending on the complexity of your personal situation. These five people may be a financial planner, an investment advisor/broker, a tax accountant, an insurance broker, and a lawyer. In many cases, multiple roles can be performed by one individual or one firm.

Frank's Recommendation

When building your advisor team, I would recommend that you start with a financial planner who can look at your situation comprehensively, and then help you identify the other key players required for your team. An independent, fee-only certified financial planner can provide you with an unbiased recommendation about the types of products, services, and advice you need to help you find and identify those individuals.

For many people, using a certified financial planner and a separate investment manager will address most of their needs. There will be times when independent legal advice will be required, but this is likely to be required only on an occasional basis.

When choosing a financial planner, ensure that he or she meets the following criteria (but remember, teams of advisors are the best):

- CFP or RFP designation
- Independent—able to make recommendations outside of the firm for which they work
- Eight or more years' comprehensive financial-planning experience
- The more designations the better

When choosing an investment advisor, ensure that he or she meets the following criteria (again, remember that teams of advisors are best):

- CFA designation
- Securities licensed and able to offer all investment products
- Independent—likely to recommend products outside the firm's products
- Eight to 10 years of experience, minimum
- The more designations the better

When choosing an insurance advisor, ensure that he or she meets the following criteria:

- CLU designation and preferably RHU as well
- Life licensed and able to offer all insurance products

- Independent broker—has access to all insurance products within the market
- A minimum of five years of experience

Antoine and Cora

Antoine and Cora contacted me because they had a problem, and they needed advice. Their problem? They had too much money. At least, that is what they were being told.

About six months earlier, Cora and Antoine had attended a seminar hosted by a local investment firm. After the presentation, they had filled out the brief questionnaire and requested more information about financial services that might be right for them. They had specified that their savings were about $900,000 and that the majority of this money was held through one of the major chartered banks.

Cora told me that since then they had received several phone calls from this investment company asking them to come in for a meeting. She had received the distinct impression from the man calling her that their account was too large to be held at a bank. That, quite simply, they had too much money to not be receiving more personalized service. I asked her whether she was happy with the service they had through their bank branch.

"Well, our representative at the bank is very nice," Cora said, "but we have had four of them over the last five years. Every time they change, we get a call from the new representative asking us to come in and review our portfolio and investment goals. When we ask them what happened to the previous person, the answer is always that they have been transferred. We dutifully go into the bank, where they ask us the same questions, with the same forms, and the whole process is pretty frustrating." I agreed that this would be frustrating and asked if they were at all worried about having that much money managed by someone they barely knew.

"Oh," she said, "we've never really thought about it that way. We assumed that since our money is invested in mutual funds with the bank that it didn't really matter who the branch advisor was—our funds are controlled by the fund managers."

"Doesn't it concern you that no one is really looking out for your money, other than you?"

"Well, that's why we're calling. The local investment firm here seems to think like you—that we're taking an awful risk by not having a consistent advisor. If you could help us decide what kind of advice we need, that would be great."

"I can absolutely help you with that."

I asked her a few more questions: Did they have a list of goals? Did they have a comprehensive financial plan? Did they know whether they had enough money for retirement? Did they feel that their lifestyle was suffering because of their dedication to saving? There is little point in sacrificing happiness in the prime of our lives for a retirement we may never experience when, with proper planning, it is usually possible to live well now and in the future. Since she wanted to work with someone local, I wished Cora success in finding the right advisor in Saskatoon, and suggested she contact at least three brokerages before making her decision. I also recommended that she contact a few investment counsel firms. Although they specialize in clients with over a million dollars in assets, their savings were so close to that milestone that I felt it was definitely worth exploring all the options. We ended our phone conversation, and I invited her to call me if she had any further questions.

I emailed Cora my list of questions for investment advisors as well as my own answers to each of the questions and general guidelines about the kinds of answers they should be looking for. For instance, any advisor they work with should have at least 10 years of experience in the industry and several designations to show a commitment to continuous learning. With an investment account of close to a million dollars, Antoine and Cora have proven that they are dedicated to their own financial future, and they deserve to be well taken care of by an experienced advisor who will be diligent with their money.

Almost a month later, Cora called and asked if it would be possible to work with me in developing a full financial plan. She explained that they had interviewed six local advisors and that, although they had all been very nice, none of them did comprehensive financial planning, and her mind had continued to return to our conversation and my focus on prioritizing and goal-setting. Plus, her friend had raved about the increase in the quality of her life and understanding of her finances since I had helped her prepare a comprehensive financial plan.

I responded that, yes, I could certainly help them with their financial planning and that I would be pleased to have a teleconference or Skype conference to explore working together more fully. We set an appointment, and I'm happy to report that, after our call, Antoine and Cora are no longer worried that they have too much money. In fact, they are now looking forward to watching their money grow even faster, with focused and experienced guidance.

Filip and Maricel

Filip emailed me to ask if I was taking new clients and explained that he was looking for a financial planner to help him and his wife, Maricel, organize their finances while they built their online business.

I arrived at the home they are renting two weeks later with the financial documents they had sent me and a list of questions I needed answered. Their three young children were getting ready for bed when I arrived, and Maricel and I talked in the kitchen while Filip read them a story. She explained that Filip had committed to reading to them every night since he had retired from his sales job. She added that he had been one of the top salespeople in his company but that the hours and travel had been hard on him. And it had been killing him to miss his children growing up.

I asked her about the online business and how that had gotten started. She admitted she had been interested in online businesses for about six years but had never found the right one . . . until Filip had decided that he wanted to switch jobs. After a lot of research, they had assembled a guide on switching careers and joined a business group where they were taught how to publish and market online. In that first year, by partnering with other companies, as well as selling their own guide, they made $40,000. The second year, they made well over $100,000, and this year it looked like they were going to earn close to $200,000. It was a phenomenal success story.

I asked, "What are you doing with the money you are earning to help build your future?"

"Well, that's the problem. We don't know what to do with it. We haven't been investing and . . ." Filip faltered. Maricel patted him on the arm and he continued, ". . . and we haven't paid our taxes for the last two years because it just all happened so quickly. We don't know where anything is, and we don't know what to do."

"It's okay," I replied, "we can deal with this. You aren't the first clients I've ever had that were behind on their taxes. Why don't you show me where you have your business papers, and we can start from there."

Maricel laughed and gestured around the room. I looked and saw boxes and shelves and cubbies full of paper—it was everywhere. They assured me that they were ready to get on top of their financial lives and to feel the relief that comes from being organized; they just needed guidance. They were in their early thirties, they had decades left in their working lives, and we all wanted to ensure that they got on the right track. At that point, they didn't know how much money they had, and even though they were earning a significant amount, it was still a challenge to make sure the bills were paid on time—which wasn't surprising, given the unopened envelopes I saw around me in the kitchen.

They started by following my recommendation to get everything organized and begin building the advisory team they needed to be successful. They interviewed three accounting firms before choosing one with bookkeepers who would come to their home. They also hired a professional organizer who could help them get their systems in place. Through a similar interview process, they found an insurance broker whom they felt comfortable with and a lawyer who could prepare their wills, powers of attorney, and personal care directives. They also found a lawyer to help with the corporate side of their lives. He helped them incorporate the business and could prepare contracts and arrange their affairs to maximize deductions by working in conjunction with their accountant. The insurance agent set them up with a group benefits package and health care spending accounts through the new corporation.

We started working through the steps I've presented to you in this book. We set goals, created a workable budget, and developed a savings and investment plan. They started setting aside money for a down payment on a home, as well as for their retirement and their children's education.

This process took several months, but Filip and Maricel were determined to put everything right. Eventually, they were ready to pay their taxes, and when I visited their home again I was pleased to see a much more organized system. Though their business required minimal time to run, they were learning that it did require time and effort to keep it organized. Filip and Maricel now have a solid team of advisors to help manage their successful business and their dreams of early retirement and financial independence.

10 Questions to Ask Your Advisor

These questions come from the Financial Planner Standards Council, which regulates the Certified Financial Planner designation.

1. What are your qualifications?
2. How many years of experience do you have?
3. What services do you offer?
4. What is your approach to financial planning? Investment management? Tax planning?
5. Will you be the only person working with me?
6. How will I pay for your services? How are you compensated?
7. How much do you typically charge?
8. Could anyone besides me benefit from your recommendations?

9. Are you regulated by any organization or agency?

10. Can I have the answers you provided in writing?

Five Questions to Ask an Advisor's Client References

1. How long have you been working with this advisor?

2. Has your experience with the advisor been positive? And why?

3. If the advisor could do more for you, what would you want or need them to do?

4. How often do you hear from the advisor? And how often would you like to hear from him or her?

5. What is one of the best experiences that you've had with this advisor and what have been the worst?

Industry-Related Sites

Financial Planner Standards Council of Canada: www.fpsc.ca

STEP Canada: The Society of Trust and Estate Practitioners: www.step.ca

The Institute of Advanced Financial Planners: www.iafp.ca

The Canadian Securities Institute: www.csi.ca

The Canadian Institute of Financial Planning: www.cifps.ca

The Canadian Securities Administrators: www.securities-administrators.ca

The Financial Advisors Association of Canada (Advocis) (Insurance): www.advocis.ca

The CFA Institute: www.cfainstitute.org

Chartered Accountants of Canada: www.cica.ca

Certified Management Accountants of Canada: www.cma-canada.org

Certified General Accountants Association of Canada: www.cga-canada.org

Chapter Summary

- Start with an independent, fee-only CFP to determine which other advisors you may need.
- Build a list of relevant advisors to your situation (planning/tax/ investments/insurance/etc.).
- Research the candidates online and through the license governing bodies.

- Download the checklists of questions to interview advisors with at www.howtoeatanelephant.ca.
- When interviewing the advisors understand:
  - how they are compensated.
  - what limitations the advisors have in the products and services they can offer you.
  - how many years of relevant experience they have.
  - their level of education and designations.
  - their approach and philosophy.
  - if you like them as person you would be willing to work with.
- Request samples of actual work they have done.
- Request at least two references.

CONCLUSION

Money is finite. If you spend it over here, you don't have it to spend over there.

—*Frank Wiginton*

CONGRATULATIONS! YOU HAVE MADE IT through to the end of this book. By now I hope that you have a much stronger understanding of personal finance and your overall personal financial situation. By dealing with your financial elephant one bite at a time, I hope you found the experience to be easy, educational, and empowering.

Now that you have a clear focus on the goals that are important to you, what resources you have, and where you can find additional income to achieve them, you will become more successful in accomplishing them.

One Frank Thought

Remember the difference between wants and needs, don't forget the guide to shopping discipline, and make your important goals the priority!

Having an understanding of your debts and knowing how to pay them out effectively will give you a tremendous feeling of direction and liberation as you start to see them paid off one by one.

Having proper living and life insurance in place to protect your income and your loved ones will provide peace of mind and security. By understanding how these work and the actual costs involved, you can save a lot of money and actually increase your overall wealth.

With a stronger understanding of what retirement is and the various ways to fund retirement, you should feel that it is much more attainable. Knowing whether or not you are likely to outlive your money and how much of an estate you are likely to leave can empower you to go after more and bigger goals!

Use the information about investing and tax planning to have intelligent, meaningful, and productive conversations with your investment advisor. By having a comprehensive financial plan, you can substantially reduce the amount of risk you *need* to take to achieve your goals.

Take a few minutes to document your wishes if something should happen to you. Use the checklists to determine who you would like to take care of things when you are able to have a conversation with them.

Lastly, take the time to interview and find the advisors whom you feel will help you achieve success in your personal finances and life. It is important that you like them and they have a good understanding of who you are and what your expectations are.

Be sure to go back to www.howtoeatanelephant.ca and review the tools you've completed online. Once you are confident that this information is correct, download a copy of the summary that pulls all the information from all the tools together into one final report.

With report in hand, I encourage you to seek out a certified financial planner who can prepare a comprehensive financial plan for you and your family. This final step will help you find additional tax savings and wealth strategies that will take your financial planning to another level and give you a better quality of life!

If you'd like to learn about the process of preparing a proper comprehensive financial plan and what you can expect from it, please go online to www.frankwiginton.com/free-e-book-on-financial-planning and download a free copy of my e-book Financial Planning—Helping You Sail Successfully Into The Future!

ABOUT THE EMPLOYEE FINANCIAL EDUCATION DIVISION

THE EMPLOYEE FINANCIAL EDUCATION DIVISION (EFED) works with businesses of all sizes to build customized employee financial education programs. Financial education programs have proven to help organizations:

- Increase productivity
- Control health care costs
- Reduce absenteeism and presenteeism
- Reduce employee stress and anxiety levels
- Decrease workplace violence and harassment
- Create greater organizational commitment
- Increase employee retention
- Increase participation in pension programs
- Help employees make better benefits choices

Most programs can be offered *at little to no cost to the company.* Programs may be as simple as pension and benefits education or more complete comprehensive financial education to all employees.

As a third party, the Employee Financial Education Division can work with your organization to help communicate financial advice to employees, thereby mitigating potential liability and reducing the workload on the Human Resources department.

These programs can be delivered through seminars, webinars, video blogs, coaching, live chat, and any other method found to be effective in reaching the employees.

Separate programs for senior management and executives can also be delivered to deal with different compensation, benefits, and pension arrangements.

Visit www.employeefinancialeducation.ca to learn more about how the Employee Financial Education Division can improve your company's bottom line.

**Employee Financial
Education Division**

INDEX

ABOUT THE AUTHOR

I truly believe that everyone can have a better quality of life through proper financial planning and advice. Finances are one of the greatest stresses in people's lives and affect everyone. If I can help you really understand your finances so you make better financial decisions, I believe you will have a better life. It's been my work life's goal to provide independent, unbiased, professional advice.

—*Frank Wiginton*

WITH 14 YEARS OF EXPERIENCE, Frank Wiginton is a highly sought after personal-finance speaker, coach, and educator who develops and delivers financial-education programs for businesses of all sizes. He works with select clients to prepare comprehensive financial plans that give them a better quality of life. Frank is often asked by the media to comment on personal finance issues. He appears as a special guest on the Business News Network (BNN), CityTV, Global Television, and CBC Radio. His advice has been quoted by the *Globe and Mail, National Post, Toronto Star, Maclean's, Canadian Business, Chatelaine,* and *MoneySense* magazine.

He is a certified financial planner (CFP), registered retirement consultant (RRC), financial management advisor (FMA), Canadian investment manager (CIM), fellow of the Canadian Securities Institute (FCSI) and FELLOW OF FPSC™.

A passionate father, sailor, traveller, photographer, and outdoorsman, Frank works and lives in the Toronto area with his wife and children.

To learn more about Frank, visit his website at www.frankwiginton.com.